SPORTS QUIZ BOOK

HarperCollins Publishers
Westerhill Road
Bishopbriggs
Glasgow
G64 2QT

First Edition 2012

Reprint 10 9 8 7 6 5 4 3 2 1 0

© HarperCollins Publishers 2012

ISBN 978-0-00-747994-8

Collins® is a registered trademark of
HarperCollins Publishers Limited

www.collinslanguage.com

A catalogue record for this book is
available from the British Library

Typeset by Davidson Publishing
Solutions, Glasgow

Printed in Great Britain by Clays Ltd,
St Ives plc

Acknowledgements
We would like to thank those authors
and publishers who kindly gave
permission for copyright material
to be used in the Collins Corpus.
We would also like to thank Times
Newspapers Ltd for providing
valuable data.

AUTHOR
Chris Bradshaw

EDITOR
Gerry Breslin
Freddy Chick

FOR THE PUBLISHER
Lucy Cooper
Julianna Dunn
Kerry Ferguson
Elaine Higgleton

Introduction

Putting his finger on what makes sport such an enjoyable thing to watch and follow, the esteemed sports writer Simon Barnes said, 'Sport is something that does not matter but is performed as if it did. In that contradiction lies its beauty.'

A knock-on effect of this is what ends up mattering to you when you are a sports fan. To the outsider these things are trivia, but to you they are essential facts. How someone played last week and what their manager thinks about them. What club a golfer is pulling out and whether they'll try hitting to the left or right of the fairway. Whether the All-Black or the Aussie pack is heavier and by how much. How many times Pietersen has got out playing a reverse sweep to left-arm spinners, how far Ryan Giggs has run in his career, how many 147 clearances there have been at the Crucible, how many of the last ten Cheltenham Gold Cup winners were Irish, how many no-hitters there have been in major league baseball, or what the average race speed is in the Tour de France. You would probably even start to care about what counts as good sumo-wrestling technique if you ever spent an afternoon watching it.

Collins Sports Quiz Book is designed to cater for this love of sports trivia and test just how much you know. It is the perfect way of seeing just which one of your friends has dedicated the most time in their lives to the back pages, and also of expanding your own knowledge a bit. There are a hundred quizzes covering everything from golf and boxing to NHL and speedway.

The quizzes

The quizzes are grouped together according to how tricky they are. First come the easy ones, then medium and finally the difficult quizzes.

Easy

Look on these as qualifying rounds. If you've got what it takes to go all the way, you should stroll through with ease. There are a couple of tougher questions in the mix that might even be labelled as 'challenging' by some judges. These have been included to add the frisson of mental sweat to an easy round.

Medium

If you're the sort of person who turns straight to the back page of a paper and only stops reading once they reach the horoscopes, then these should be easy. Lesser sports fanatics should find these a good challenge and will be doing well to get them right.

Difficult

These are a mental Olympiad. The bar is set high. Anyone who is getting these consistently right should be regarded suspiciously. Ask to see their smartphone's browser history.

The answers

The answers to each quiz are printed at the end of the following quiz. For example, the answers to Quiz 1: Pot Luck appear at the bottom of Quiz 2: Athletics. The exception to this rule is the last quiz in every level. The answers to these quizzes appear at the end of the very first quiz in the level.

Running a quiz

Collins Sports Quiz Book is only half-finished. (Wait! Don't demand a refund yet, read on!) People don't go to the theatre to sit and read a script. Likewise, the quizzes in this book need someone to read them out. That's you.

If you're just quizzing your family during a car journey, or your mates of an afternoon, then there's probably no need to put in lots of preparation. If you're planning on using this book to run a more organized and formal quiz, however, there are a few things you need to get right before you start:

🏁 Rehearse: don't just pick this book up and read out the questions cold. Go through all the quizzes you're going to use by yourself beforehand. Note down all the questions (notes look better in a quiz environment than reading from a book) and answers. Although every effort has been made to ensure that all the answers in *Collins Sports Quiz Book* are correct, despite our best endeavours, mistakes may still appear. If you see an answer you are not sure is right, or if you think there is more than one possible answer, then check.

🏁 Paper and writing implements: do yourself a favour and prepare enough sheets of paper for everyone to write on. The aim of the game here is to stop the mad impulse certain people feel to 'help'. They will spend ten minutes running around looking for 'scrap' paper, probably ripping up your latest novel in the process. The same problem applies to pens. Ideally, have enough for everyone. Remember, though, that over half of them will be lost forever once you've given them out. You can use the 'Keeping Score' pages at the back of the book to record the quiz scores for each team or person.

🏁 Prizes: everyone likes a prize. Since this is a sports quiz book, your audience will probably not understand the concept of a competition without one. No matter how small, it's best to have one on offer.

Good luck! We hope you enjoy *Collins Sports Quiz Book*.

Contents

Easy Quizzes

Medium Quizzes

Difficult Quizzes

EASY QUIZZES

Quiz 1: Pot Luck

1. Who won the Premier League in 2012?

2. The British Formula One Grand Prix is held at which circuit?

3. The Big Easy is the nickname of which golfer?

4. Which county cricket team play their home games at Lord's?

5. What was the name of the stadium that hosted the athletics events at the 2008 Olympic Games?

6. Who was the first triple jumper to break the 60ft barrier?

7. What nationality is football manager José Mourinho?

8. Who did Chelsea beat in the 2012 Champions League final?

9. Which dart player is known as The Power?

10. How long is a rugby union pitch?

11. Turf Moor is the home ground of which football club?

12. The Stoop is the home ground of which rugby union team?

13. In rugby league, how many points are awarded for a drop goal?

14. Sainte Dévote, Massenet and Mirabeau Bas are features of which Formula One circuit?

15. What is the oldest of golf's four majors?

16. Who announced his retirement after a heavy defeat at the 2012 World Snooker Championship?

17. How many flights must an athlete clear in an Olympic 400m hurdles race?

18. Each innings in a Cricket World Cup match lasts how many overs?

19. Which team won the Spanish Primera División in 2012?
    a) Barcelona
    b) Real Madrid
    c) Atlético Madrid

20. Who finished bottom of the Premier League in 2011/12?
    a) Blackburn
    b) Bolton
    c) Wolverhampton Wanderers

Answers to Quiz 33: Pot Luck

1. New Delhi
2. Germany
3. Swansea City
4. Solheim Cup
5. The Netherlands
6. Northamptonshire
7. Jonathan Edwards
8. Fijian
9. Croke Park
10. Didier Drogba
11. London Irish
12. Copa Libertadores
13. Tanni Grey-Thompson
14. Dundee United
15. Aintree
16. Portugal
17. Virginia Wade
18. Venus Williams
19. Trinidad and Tobago
20. 1998

Quiz 2: Athletics

1. Who won the men's 5,000m at the 2011 World Championships?

2. Who was the first athlete to successfully defend the men's 1,500m at the Olympics?

3. What is the first event of the women's heptathlon?

4. Who is the oldest male athlete to win the Olympic 100 metres?

5. Dai Greene won a gold medal at the 2011 World Championships in which event?

6. Who holds the women's 100m world record?

7. In what event do Chris Tomlinson and Greg Rutherford compete?

8. Who is the only woman to hold the World, Olympic, European and Commonwealth 400m hurdles titles at the same time?

9. Whose 200m world record did Usain Bolt break at the 2008 Olympics?

10. Who won the heptathlon gold medal at the 2009 World Athletics Championships?

11. David Hemery won Olympic gold at which event?

12. In which Scandinavian city is the annual Bislett Games meeting held?

13. Kelly Sotherton won Olympic and World Championship medals at which event?

14. What is the longest Olympic track event?

15. Jan Železný was a world and Olympic gold medallist at which event?

16. Who was the only British athlete to win a field event medal at the 2011 World Championships?

17. Who won the gold medal in the men's 800m at the 1980 Moscow Olympics?

18. What is the penultimate event of a decathlon?

19. Which Jamaican won the men's 100m at the 2011 World Championships?
    a) Yohan Blake
    b) Usain Bolt
    c) Asafa Powell

20. How often does the World Athletics Championships take place?
    a) every year
    b) every 2 years
    c) every 4 years

EASY

Answers to Quiz 1: Pot Luck

1. Manchester City
2. Silverstone
3. Ernie Els
4. Middlesex
5. The Bird's Nest
6. Jonathan Edwards
7. Portuguese
8. Bayern Munich
9. Phil Taylor
10. 100m
11. Burnley
12. Harlequins
13. One
14. Monaco
15. The Open Championship
16. Stephen Hendry
17. 10
18. 50
19. Real Madrid
20. Wolverhampton Wanderers

Quiz 3: Pot Luck

EASY

1. Which two teams contest the Australian State of Origin rugby league series?

2. What is Tiger Woods' real first name?

3. Kenilworth Road is the home ground of which football club?

4. What nationality is boxing champion Manny Pacquiao?

5. Who won the US Open men's singles title every year from 2004 until 2008?

6. Silverback is the nickname of which dart player?

7. In what month does the third round of the FA Cup usually take place?

8. Joe Cole spent the 2011/12 season playing for which French club?

9. How many players make up a beach volleyball team?

10. Which county cricket team play their home games at the Rose Bowl?

11. Which rugby union club did Jason Robinson join after he left rugby league's Wigan Warriors?

12. The Real Deal is the nickname of which World Heavyweight Champion?

13. Who was the first black British woman to win an Olympic gold medal?

14. Craven Park is the home ground of which rugby league team?

15. Which city hosted the 2012 Champions League final?

16. Premier League footballer Ryan Nelsen plays international football for which country?

17. On a standard dartboard what number lies between 4 and 6?

18. The 1908 London Olympics were hosted at which stadium?

19. How many players were in the final squads in each UEFA Euro 2012 squad?
    a) 22
    b) 23
    c) 24

20. Robin van Persie joined Arsenal from which Dutch club?
    a) Ajax
    b) Feyenoord
    c) Willem II

Answers to Quiz 2: Athletics

1. Mo Farah	11. 400m hurdles
2. Seb Coe	12. Oslo
3. 100m hurdles	13. Heptathlon
4. Linford Christie	14. 10,000m
5. 400m hurdles	15. Javelin
6. Florence Griffith-Joyner	16. Phillips Idowu
7. Long jump	17. Steve Ovett
8. Sally Gunnell	18. Javelin
9. Michael Johnson	19. Yohan Blake
10. Jessica Ennis	20. Every 2 years

Quiz 4: Boxing

1. Which pair of British fighters were involved in a press conference brawl after a 2012 World Championship fight?

2. Who beat Amir Khan in a controversial world title fight in Washington in December 2011?

3. Which giant Russian did David Haye beat to claim the WBA world heavyweight championship in 2009?

4. Who in 2005 became the first British boxer to be named Ring Magazine Fighter of the Year?

5. Ricky Hatton's only two professional defeats were at the hands of which fighters?

6. Who is the youngest man to win the world heavyweight championship?

7. What nationality are boxing's Klitschko brothers?

8. Who is the only World Heavyweight Champion to retire undefeated?

9. The Cobra is the nickname of which British World Champion?

10. What belt is awarded to winners of British title fights?

11. Which 50/1 outsider shocked Lennox Lewis in a 2001 heavyweight championship fight?

12. Which Irish super middleweight appeared in the video to the U2 song Sweetest Thing?

13. The Dark Destroyer was the nickname of which British soldier turned fighter?

14. Which Welsh fighter lost a world cruiserweight title unification contest against David Haye in 2008?

15. Which fighter was elected to the House of Representatives of the Philippines in 2010?

16. Which British superheavyweight won gold at the 2000 Olympic Games?

17. Golden Boy is the nickname of which fighter?

18. Which Mexican's run of 87 consecutive wins, which stretched back to 1980, was brought to an end by Pernell Whitaker in 1993?

19. How many fights did Joe Calzaghe lose in his professional career?
    a) none
    b) one
    c) two

20. What is the minimum weight in pounds for a heavyweight fighter?
    a) 190lb
    b) 200lb
    c) 210lb

Answers to Quiz 3: Pot Luck

1. Queensland and New South Wales
2. Eldrick
3. Luton Town
4. Filipino
5. Roger Federer
6. Tony O'Shea
7. January
8. Lille
9. 2
10. Hampshire
11. Sale Sharks
12. Evander Holyfield
13. Tessa Sanderson
14. Hull Kingston Rovers
15. Munich
16. New Zealand
17. 13
18. White City Stadium
19. 23
20. Feyenoord

Quiz 5: Pot Luck

1. Which four field events feature in an Olympic heptathlon?

2. Amy Williams won a gold medal at the 2010 Winter Olympics in which event?

3. Who did Paul Lambert succeed as manager of Aston Villa?

4. The Augusta National Golf Club is in which American state?

5. Which Australian batsman is nicknamed Mr Cricket?

6. Which German club finished runners-up in the Bundesliga, the German Cup and the Champions League in 2012?

7. Which Pakistani all-rounder smashed a century off just 37 balls against Sri Lanka in 1996?

8. UK athletics chief Charles van Commenee was involved in a row in 2011 with which athlete about the use of Twitter?

9. Which rugby league team are nicknamed the Vikings?

10. Who lit the Olympic Flame at the 2000 Sydney Games?

11. Which clanger-prone Manchester United goalkeeper was nicknamed The Blind Venetian?

12. Who was the first batsman to score 13,000 Test runs?

13. Who was the first host of TV quiz show A Question of Sport?

14. What are the two teams in cricket's County Championship that start with the letter D?

15. Which Manchester City player was banned for 6 months in 2011 after failing a drugs test?

16. Who, in 2006, became the first Englishman to score in three consecutive World Cups?

17. Who is the only Frenchman to have won the Formula One Drivers' Championship?

18. What is the only city to host the Summer Olympic Games three times?

19. England cricket coach Andy Flower played international cricket for which country?
    a) New Zealand
    b) South Africa
    c) Zimbabwe

20. Who were the first winners of the Rugby World Cup?
    a) Australia
    b) New Zealand
    c) South Africa

Answers to Quiz 4: Boxing

1. David Haye and Dereck Chisora
2. Lamont Peterson
3. Nikolay Valuev
4. Ricky Hatton
5. Floyd Mayweather Jr and Manny Pacquiao
6. Mike Tyson
7. Ukrainian
8. Rocky Marciano
9. Carl Froch
10. Lonsdale Belt
11. Hasim Rahman
12. Steve Collins
13. Nigel Benn
14. Enzo Maccarinelli
15. Manny Pacquiao
16. Audley Harrison
17. Oscar de la Hoya
18. Julio Cesar Chavez
19. None
20. 200lb

Quiz 6: Cricket

EASY

1. England captain Andrew Strauss plays county cricket for which team?

2. Who is the leading wicket taker in the history of Test cricket?

3. Who captained the England side that won the World Twenty20 in 2010?

4. Who, in 2012, became the seventh England player to appear on both the batting and bowling honours boards at Lord's?

5. The Gabba is in which Australian city?

6. Who scored 294 in a Test match against India at Edgbaston in 2011?

7. The Turbanator is the nickname of which spin bowler?

8. Who scored a century on his Test debut against Australia in the 2009 Ashes decider at The Oval?

9. Which England cricketer was nicknamed the King of Spain?

10. Who captained India to victory in the 2011 Cricket World Cup final?

11. The Proteas is the nickname of which international cricket team?

12. Headingley Carnegie is the home ground of which county cricket team?

13. Who is England's all-time leading Test run scorer?

14. Who is England's all-time leading Test wicket taker?

15. Which batsman succeeded Ricky Ponting as captain of the Australian Test team?

16. Who was the leading wicket taker in the 2010/11 Ashes series?

17. Which country reached the Cricket World Cup final in 1979, 1987 and 1992?

18. Kumar Sangakkara and Rangana Herath play international cricket for which country?

19. Who was the first batsman to score 100 international centuries?
    a) Don Bradman
    b) Brian Lara
    c) Sachin Tendulkar

20. What was England's winning margin in the 2010/11 Ashes series?
    a) 2-1
    b) 3-0
    c) 3-1

Answers to Quiz 5: Pot Luck

1. High jump, shot put, long jump and javelin
2. Skeleton
3. Alex McLeish
4. Georgia
5. Mike Hussey
6. Bayern Munich
7. Shahid Afridi
8. Phillips Idowu
9. Widnes
10. Cathy Freeman
11. Massimo Taibi
12. Sachin Tendulkar
13. David Vine
14. Derbyshire and Durham
15. Kolo Touré
16. David Beckham
17. Alain Prost
18. London
19. Zimbabwe
20. New Zealand

Quiz 7: Pot Luck

1. Which constructor has won the most Grand Prix races since the start of Formula One?

2. Which golfer is nicknamed El Niño?

3. What was the first Asian city to host the Summer Olympics?

4. Which two countries that hosted a Formula One race in 2012 start with the letter M?

5. Who resigned as Barcelona manager at the end of the 2011/12 season?

6. Which West Indian fast bowler was known as Whispering Death?

7. A slob unit is an anagram of which athlete?

8. Odsal Stadium is the home ground of which rugby league team?

9. At which course is the classic horse race The Oaks run?

10. Where did Wales play home rugby internationals prior to moving to the Millennium Stadium?

11. How many players are on a hockey team?

12. Which British rider broke his collarbone after a fall in the 2011 Tour de France?

13. The 2022 World Cup will be hosted in which Asian country?

14. At what racecourse is the Prix de l'Arc de Triomphe run?

15. The Holte End is a stand at which football ground?

16. Which famous footballing figure is the owner of the 2,000 Guineas winning horse Rock of Gibraltar?

17. The Marina Bay Street Circuit is the venue for which Formula One Grand Prix?

18. What connects the band Coldplay and the New Zealand cricket team?

19. The Boston Bruins participate in which sport?
    a) baseball
    b) basketball
    c) ice hockey

20. Which field event is not part of a decathlon?
    a) discus
    b) hammer
    c) shot put

EASY

Answers to Quiz 6: Cricket

1.	Middlesex	11.	South Africa
2.	Muttiah Muralitharan	12.	Yorkshire
3.	Paul Collingwood	13.	Graham Gooch
4.	Stuart Broad	14.	Ian Botham
5.	Brisbane	15.	Michael Clarke
6.	Alastair Cook	16.	James Anderson
7.	Harbhajan Singh	17.	England
8.	Jonathan Trott	18.	Sri Lanka
9.	Ashley Giles	19.	Sachin Tendulkar
10.	Mahendra Singh Dhoni	20.	3-1

Quiz 8: Cycling

1. Who has won the Tour de France the most times?

2. Which cyclist won the BBC Sports Personality of the Year award in 2011?

3. In the Tour de France, the polka dot jersey is worn by the leader of which competition?

4. The last stage of the Tour de France always takes place in which city?

5. What jersey is worn by a World Champion cyclist?

6. Which British rider came fourth in the 2009 Tour de France?

7. Who, in 2011, became the first Australian to win the Tour de France?

8. Which Scot broke the one hour speed record riding a bike nicknamed 'Old Faithful'?

9. Which Frenchman, who died in 2010, won the Tour de France in 1983 and 1984?

10. Which British rider won three gold medals at the 2008 Olympic Games?

11. Over what distance is the track cycling Olympic Team Pursuit run?

12. What nationality are cycling's Schlek brothers?

13. Which Italian sprinter was nicknamed Super Mario?

14. Which rider died on the ascent of Mont Ventoux during the 1967 Tour de France?

15. The prologue for the 2007 Tour de France was staged in which city?

16. The Pirate was the nickname of which Italian climber who won the Tour de France in 1998?

17. Who won the women's road race at the 2008 Olympic Games?

18. What colour jersey is worn by the leader of the Giro D'Italia?

19. How many riders are there in each team in the Tour de France?
    a) 8
    b) 9
    c) 10

20. Who is the only Irish rider to win the Tour de France?
    a) Sean Kelly
    b) Paul Kimmage
    c) Stephen Roche

Answers to Quiz 7: Pot Luck

1. Ferrari
2. Sergio Garcia
3. Tokyo
4. Monaco and Malaysia
5. Pep Guardiola
6. Michael Holding
7. Usain Bolt
8. Bradford Bulls
9. Epsom
10. Cardiff Arms Park
11. 11
12. Bradley Wiggins
13. Qatar
14. Longchamp
15. Villa Park
16. Sir Alex Ferguson
17. The Singapore Grand Prix
18. They both have members called Chris Martin
19. Ice hockey
20. Hammer

Quiz 9: Pot Luck

1. Which Classic horse race was won by Frankel in 2011?

2. Which sport has provided the most winners of the BBC Sports Personality of the Year award?

3. Who was the first footballer to be sent off twice for the England football team?

4. Which footballer was fined by UEFA for revealing a shirt in support of striking dock workers after scoring in a 1997 European Cup Winners' Cup tie?

5. Which veteran Danish golfer finished in fourth place in the 2011 Open Championship?

6. Who shocked Eric Bristow in the 1983 World Darts Championship final?

7. Which South African won golf's US Masters in 2011?

8. Who did José Mourinho succeed as manager of Chelsea?

9. At what circuit does the Italian Formula One grand prix take place?

10. The Road Hole is a feature of which golf course?

11. Neil Lennon succeeded which Englishman as manager of Celtic?

12. In a Formula One race, what flag is flown to indicate that drivers should slow down and that overtaking is banned?

13. Jackpot is the nickname of which dart player?

14. How many players can a team have on the ice at any one time in an ice hockey game?

15. In rugby league, how many points are awarded for a try?

16. Who was the manager of the 2012 Great Britain Olympic football team?

17. No unbent jots is an anagram of which racing driver?

18. The Australian Open tennis tournament takes place in which city?

19. Which World Cup winner's shirt fetched £157,750 at auction in 2002?
    a) Diego Maradona
    b) Bobby Moore
    c) Pelé

20. Boxer Ricky Hatton is a fan of which football club?
    a) Manchester City
    b) Manchester United
    c) Liverpool

Answers to Quiz 8: Cycling

1. Lance Armstrong
2. Mark Cavendish
3. The King of the Mountains
4. Paris
5. Rainbow jersey
6. Bradley Wiggins
7. Cadel Evans
8. Graeme Obree
9. Laurent Fignon
10. Chris Hoy
11. 4,000m
12. Luxembourger
13. Mario Cipollini
14. Tom Simpson
15. London
16. Marco Pantani
17. Nicole Cook
18. Pink
19. 9
20. Stephen Roche

Quiz 10: Darts

EASY

1. Which player won the 2012 PDC World Championship?

2. Who won the 2012 BDO equivalent?

3. Which player has won the World Championship the most times?

4. The Count is the nickname of which player?

5. The finals of both the BDO and PDC World Championship are the best of how many sets?

6. Who is the only player to have won the PDC World Darts Championship but not the BDO equivalent?

7. True or false – football legend George Best once appeared on darting game show Bullseye?

8. The final of the 2012 Premier League Darts was held at which London venue?

9. Who was the first player to win the BDO and PDC versions of the World Championship?

10. Which former World Champion died in March 2012?

11. In addition to Phil Taylor, which two players have five World Championships to their name?

12. Who are the two players to hit a nine-dart finish at the PDC World Championship?

13. What do the initials PDC stand for?

14. Which player is nicknamed Wolfie?

15. Who was the first player to hit a nine-dart finish at the Lakeside BDO World Championship?

16. Old Stoneface was the title of which player's autobiography?

17. Which hairy player lost in the final of the BDO World Championship in 2009 and 2012?

18. Who hit two nine-dart finishes in the final of the 2010 Premier League?

19. What was the venue for the 2012 PDC World Championship?
    a) Alexandra Palace
    b) Circus Tavern, Purfleet
    c) Wembley Arena

20. Phil Taylor, Adrian Lewis and Ted Hankey are all from which city?
    a) Leicester
    b) Nottingham
    c) Stoke-on-Trent

Answers to Quiz 9: Pot Luck

1. 2,000 Guineas
2. Athletics
3. David Beckham
4. Robbie Fowler
5. Thomas Björn
6. Keith Deller
7. Charl Schwartzel
8. Claudio Ranieri
9. Monza
10. St Andrews
11. Tony Mowbray
12. Yellow
13. Adrian Lewis
14. 6
15. 4
16. Stuart Pearce
17. Jenson Button
18. Melbourne
19. Pelé
20. Manchester City

Quiz 11: Pot Luck

EASY

1. What nationality is Formula One driver Sebastian Vettel?

2. Which 100/1 outsider won the 2009 Grand National?

3. What name connects the Governor of the Bank of England, a darts champion and a bowls champion?

4. Who is the only Spaniard to have won the Formula One Drivers' Championship?

5. In January 2012, who became the third batsman to score 13,000 Test match runs?

6. At what circuit is the Portuguese Formula One Grand Prix held?

7. Who missed a last-minute penalty for Ghana against Uruguay in a 2010 World Cup quarter-final?

8. Which Belarussian tennis player won the Women's Singles at the 2012 Australian Open?

9. Who did Alan Pardew succeed as manager of Newcastle United?

10. What is the name of the Indian Premier League cricket team in Delhi?

11. Which country finished third at the World Cup in both 2006 and 2010?

12. Tattenham Corner is a feature of which racecourse?

13. Boundary Park is the home ground of which English football club?

14. Who is South Africa's youngest Test cricket captain?

15. Over what distance is the Olympic steeplechase run?

16. At which sport can a player score a turkey?

17. Pacman is the nickname of which multiple world champion boxer?

18. Which African team did England face at the 2010 World Cup?

19. Who whistled his way through the national anthem after winning gold at the 1984 Olympic Games?
    a) Seb Coe
    b) Steve Ovett
    c) Daley Thompson

20. Small Heath Alliance was the original name of which English football club?
    a) Aston Villa
    b) Birmingham City
    c) West Bromwich Albion

Answers to Quiz 10: Darts

1. Adrian Lewis
2. Christian Kist
3. Phil Taylor
4. Ted Hankey
5. 13
6. Adrian Lewis
7. True
8. O2 Arena
9. Dennis Priestley
10. Jocky Wilson
11. Eric Bristow and Raymond van Barneveld
12. Raymond van Barneveld and Adrian Lewis
13. Professional Darts Corporation
14. Martin Adams
15. Paul Lim
16. John Lowe
17. Tony O'Shea
18. Phil Taylor
19. Alexandra Palace
20. Stoke-on-Trent

Quiz 12: Football

1. Who scored the winning penalty for Chelsea in the Champions League final shoot-out in 2012?

2. Sir Geoff Hurst scored a hat trick in the 1966 World Cup final. Who scored England's other goal?

3. Who is the only man to have played and scored in each of the first 20 Premier League seasons?

4. What nationality is Manchester City captain Vincent Kompany?

5. Who was the first foreign manager to lead a team to victory in the FA Cup final?

6. Who were the first British winners of the European Cup?

7. Manchester United beat which team 8-2 in the 2011/12 Premier League season?

8. Who was the first midfielder to score 150 Premier League goals?

9. Which country won the first World Cup?

10. The Kassam Stadium is the home ground of which English club?

11. What animal made an appearance on the pitch during Blackburn's 2012 Premier League game against Wigan?

12. Ivanhoe is the middle name of which much travelled England striker?

13. England won just one game at the 2010 World Cup. Who did they beat?

14. Which two managers have led Chelsea to the Premier League title?

15. Which team won the League Cup in 2011 but were relegated from the Premier League later that season?

16. Demba Ba and Papiss Cissé play international football for which country?

17. Home Park is the home ground of which English football club?

18. Which country hosted the 2010 World Cup?

19. Who is the leading Premier League goal scorer?
    a) Andy Cole
    b) Thierry Henry
    c) Alan Shearer

20. Which of the following countries wasn't in England's Euro 2012 group?
    a) Poland
    b) Sweden
    c) Ukraine

Answers to Quiz 11: Pot Luck

1. German
2. Mon Mome
3. Mervyn King
4. Fernando Alonso
5. Ricky Ponting
6. Estoril
7. Asamoah Gyan
8. Victoria Azarenka
9. Chris Hughton
10. Daredevils

11. Germany
12. Epsom
13. Oldham Athletic
14. Graeme Smith
15. 3,000m
16. Ten-pin bowling
17. Manny Pacquiao
18. Algeria
19. Daley Thompson
20. Birmingham City

Quiz 13: Pot Luck

1. Which two English classic horse races are open to fillies only?

2. Who scored the injury-time goal that sealed the Premier League title for Manchester City in the last game of the 2011/12 season?

3. The Wall is the nickname of which obdurate Indian batsman?

4. Which of golf's majors takes place earliest in the year?

5. In rugby league, what number shirt does the full back wear?

6. In motorsport, what do the initials FIA stand for?

7. What sporting event is nicknamed La Grande Boucle?

8. Which country reached the World Cup final in four tournaments out of five between 1974 and 1990?

9. What colour is the central segment of an archery target?

10. Who was the manager of the England football team at Euro 2000?

11. Yeongam is the venue for the Formula One Grand Prix in which country?

12. Which country hosted the first football World Cup?

13. How long is an NFL American football pitch from goal line to goal line?

14. Langtree Park is the home ground of which rugby league team?

15. Roy Hodgson left which club to take the England manager's job?

16. What number lies between 16 and 19 on a standard dartboard?

17. In what year was the first Rugby World Cup held?

18. Gary Cahill joined Chelsea from which club?

19. What number shirt was worn by Chicago Bulls basketball legend Michael Jordan?
    a) 7
    b) 13
    c) 23

20. In rugby league, how many points are awarded for a penalty kick?
    a) 1
    b) 2
    c) 3

Answers to Quiz 12: Football

1. Didier Drogba
2. Martin Peters
3. Ryan Giggs
4. Belgian
5. Ruud Gullit
6. Celtic
7. Arsenal
8. Frank Lampard
9. Uruguay
10. Oxford United
11. Chicken
12. Emile Heskey
13. Slovenia
14. José Mourinho and Carlo Ancelotti
15. Birmingham City
16. Senegal
17. Plymouth Argyle
18. South Africa
19. Alan Shearer
20. Poland

Quiz 14: Formula One

1. Which driver won the 2011 World Drivers' Championship?

2. Which Grand Prix takes place at the Nurburgring?

3. Who were McLaren's two drivers for the 2012 season?

4. Which team won the Constructors' Championship in 2011?

5. The opening race of the 2012 season took place in which country?

6. Who did Lewis Hamilton overtake on the last lap of the last race to clinch the 2008 Drivers' Championship?

7. Which country hosted its first Grand Prix in October 2011?

8. Who are the three Brazilians to have won the Drivers' Championship?

9. How many points did the fourth place finisher in a race receive during the 2012 season?

10. Name the six former World Champions who took part in the 2012 season.

11. In terms of races won, who is Britain's most successful Formula One driver?

12. Who has won the Formula One Drivers' Championship the most times?

13. Jenson Button won the 2009 Drivers' Championship with which team?

14. What colour flag is waved to indicate an accident or poor track conditions?

15. Who is the youngest man to win the Drivers' Championship?

16. What relation is Bruno Senna to the late Ayrton Senna?

17. Which driver won the Monaco Grand Prix five years in a row from 1989 to 1993?

18. The Yas Marina Circuit is the home to which Grand Prix?

19. How many races were scheduled for the 2012 season?
    a) 18
    b) 19
    c) 20

20. How many points does the winning driver of a Grand Prix receive?
    a) 10
    b) 15
    c) 25

Answers to Quiz 13: Pot Luck

1. The Oaks and The 1,000 Guineas
2. Sergio Agüero
3. Rahul Dravid
4. The US Masters
5. 1
6. Fédération Internationale de l'Automobile
7. Tour de France
8. West Germany
9. Gold (also accept yellow)
10. Kevin Keegan
11. South Korea
12. Uruguay
13. 100 yards
14. St Helens
15. West Bromwich Albion
16. 7
17. 1987
18. Bolton Wanderers
19. 23
20. 2

Quiz 15: Pot Luck

EASY

1. Which three horse races make up the English triple crown?

2. Prior to 2012, in what year did Manchester City last win the top flight?

3. True or false – Formula One racer Jenson Button failed his first driving test?

4. Who is the only Newcastle United boss to win the Premier League Manager of the Season award?

5. Which team finished fourth in the 2010 World Cup?

6. In what year did Coventry City win their only FA Cup final?

7. Noted for his bushy beard, who was the first player of Indian ancestry to play Test cricket for South Africa?

8. Which two countries have won the Rugby World Cup on home soil?

9. Who, in 2010, became the first German golfer to win the US PGA?

10. The Bronzed Adonis is the nickname of which handsome dart player?

11. What do the initials BBBC stand for?

12. What was the first European country to host the World Cup?

13. What are the eight countries to have won football's World Cup?

14. Or cry mr oily is an anagram of which golfer?

15. Ryan Giggs' father was a professional at which sport?

16. Which team won the Formula One Constructors' Championship in 2010?

17. Which jockey has won The Derby the most times?

18. What name connects an MP who has campaigned against phone hacking and a champion golfer?

19. How many teams took part in the 2010 World Cup?
    a) 24
    b) 28
    c) 32

20. What was the first country to win the Rugby World Cup twice?
    a) Australia
    b) New Zealand
    c) South Africa

EASY

Answers to Quiz 14: Formula One

1. Sebastian Vettel
2. German
3. Lewis Hamilton and Jenson Button
4. Red Bull
5. Australia
6. Timo Glock
7. India
8. Emerson Fittipaldi, Nelson Piquet and Ayrton Senna
9. 12
10. Sebastian Vettel, Jenson Button, Lewis Hamilton, Kimi Räikkönen, Fernando Alonso and Michael Schumacher

11. Nigel Mansell
12. Michael Schumacher
13. Brawn GP
14. Red flag
15. Sebastian Vettel
16. Nephew
17. Ayrton Senna
18. Abu Dhabi
19. 20
20. 25

Quiz 16: Golf

1. Which left-hander won The Masters in 2012?

2. What is the name of the trophy awarded to the winner of the Open Championship?

3. Who became the first European to win the US Open in 40 years after winning at Pebble Beach in 2010?

4. Which Englishman has made the most appearances in the Ryder Cup?

5. What is the last major of the year?

6. Who holds the record for the most consecutive European PGA Tour Order of Merit wins?

7. What bird is used to describe scoring three strokes under par for a hole?

8. Who won the US Masters in 2004, 2006 and 2010?

9. Which Northern Irishman won the 2011 Open Championship?

10. What is the most successful partnership in the history of the Ryder Cup?

11. Which course has hosted The Open Championship the most times?

12. True or false – no golfer who has won the par-three contest at Augusta has won The Masters in the same year?

13. Which Briton won the Order of Merit in both Europe and the USA in 2011?

14. In what country was Justin Rose born?

15. Who was the first golfer from the Republic of Ireland to win The Open Championship?

16. Which Swede won the European Order of Merit in 2008?

17. Who are the two Germans to win majors?

18. Who has won the US Masters the most times?

19. Players on the European Tour compete in the Race To...?
    a) Dubai
    b) Oman
    c) Singapore

20. What colour jacket is awarded to the winner of the US Masters?
    a) Blue
    b) Green
    c) Pink

Answers to Quiz 15: Pot Luck

1. The Derby, The 2,000 Guineas and The St Leger
2. 1968
3. True
4. Alan Pardew
5. Uruguay
6. 1987
7. Hashim Amla
8. New Zealand and South Africa
9. Martin Kaymer
10. Steve Beaton
11. British Boxing Board of Control
12. Italy
13. Uruguay, Italy, France, Brazil, Germany, England, Argentina and Spain
14. Rory McIlroy
15. Rugby league
16. Red Bull-Renault
17. Lester Piggott
18. Tom Watson
19. 32
20. Australia

Quiz 17: Pot Luck

1. What road do the horses cross en route to the first fence of the Grand National?

2. What was the only tennis major that Pete Sampras did not win?

3. A speedway race takes place over how many laps?

4. Who has scored the most tries in the history of the Rugby World Cup?

5. Who was the first woman golfer to be invited to play on the men's European Tour?

6. Which Englishman refereed the 2010 World Cup final?

7. Which cricketer is nicknamed the Rawalpindi Express?

8. Before moving to the Riverside Stadium, what was Middlesbrough's home ground?

9. Who in 2012 became only the second side to defend rugby's Heineken Cup?

10. Ireland thrashed England 43-13 in the 2007 Six Nations Championship. Where was the match played?

11. Which wonder horse won The Derby in 1981 by 10 lengths?

12. Which driver holds the record for the most Formula One Grand Prix wins?

13. Brian Lara enjoyed a record-breaking spell with which English county cricket team?

14. Which London venue hosts the pre-Wimbledon AEGON Tennis Championships?

15. Who won four gold medals at the 1936 Olympic Games?

16. Which manager gave his team a half-time dressing down on the pitch in a 2008 game against Manchester City?

17. Who was sent off in Chelsea's 2011/12 Champions League semi-final against Barcelona?

18. Who did Nigel Adkins succeed as manager of Southampton?

19. Who is the coach of the Irish rugby union team?
    a) Declan Heart
    b) Declan Kidney
    c) Declan Liver

20. The Chinese Formula One Grand Prix takes place in which city?
    a) Beijing
    b) Shanghai
    c) Shenzhen

Answers to Quiz 16: Golf

1. Bubba Watson
2. The Claret Jug
3. Graeme McDowell
4. Nick Faldo
5. US PGA
6. Colin Montgomerie
7. Albatross
8. Phil Mickelson
9. Darren Clarke
10. Seve Ballesteros and José María Olazábal
11. St Andrews
12. True
13. Luke Donald
14. South Africa
15. Padraig Harrington
16. Robert Karlsson
17. Bernhard Langer and Martin Kaymer
18. Jack Nicklaus
19. Dubai
20. Green

Quiz 18: Horse Racing

1. The Derby is held at which course?

2. What is Frankie Dettori's real first name?

3. In what month does the Cheltenham Festival take place?

4. Who was the Champion Flat Jockey in 2010 and 2011?

5. Choc is the nickname of which jockey?

6. Who was the National Hunt Champion Trainer every season from 2005/06 to 2011/12?

7. On what day of the year is the King George VI Chase usually run?

8. Which Cheltenham Gold Cup winning horse was killed at the 2012 Grand National?

9. Which horse won the 2011 Derby but never raced again?

10. The Eclipse Stakes is run at which course?

11. What was the first horse to regain the Cheltenham Gold Cup?

12. Tony McCoy won his first Grand National in 2010 riding which horse?

13. Which horse won a hat-trick of Cheltenham Gold Cups in 2002, 2003 and 2004?

14. Which jockey rode the most winners at the Cheltenham Festival in 2006, 2008, 2009, 2010 and 2011?

15. At what course is the Lincoln Handicap run?

16. What horse won the 2012 Grand National?

17. The Welsh Grand National is run at which course?

18. Which horse won the World Hurdle at the Cheltenham Festival for the fourth consecutive time in 2012?

19. How many fences do the runners jump in the Grand National?
    a) 28
    b) 30
    c) 32

20. Who is the only jockey to win the BBC Sports Personality of the Year award?
    a) Willie Carson
    b) Tony McCoy
    c) Lester Piggott

EASY

Answers to Quiz 17: Pot Luck

1. Melling Road
2. French Open
3. 4
4. Jonah Lomu
5. Michelle Wie
6. Howard Webb
7. Shoaib Akhtar
8. Ayresome Park
9. Leinster
10. Croke Park
11. Shergar
12. Michael Schumacher
13. Warwickshire
14. Queen's Club
15. Jesse Owens
16. Phil Brown
17. John Terry
18. Alan Pardew
19. Declan Kidney
20. Shanghai

Quiz 19: Pot Luck

1. Which racing driver has been honoured on Birmingham's Walk of Stars?

2. In what month does the Australian Open tennis championship take place?

3. Over how many furlongs is The Derby run?

4. Which of the home nations was beaten by Western Samoa at the 1991 Rugby World Cup?

5. How many riders take part in a speedway race?

6. Which two French teams have taken part in rugby league's Super League?

7. Which player held up a banner saying 'RIP Fergie' during Manchester City's Premier League victory celebration?

8. The main stadium at the US Open tennis is named after which player?

9. Who scored his 3,000th point for St Helens in their 31-18 win over Leeds in May 2012?

10. Which rugby player was dismissed by Cardiff Blues in 2012 after an alcohol-related incident on a plane?

11. Who are the two players to have made more than one maximum break at the World Snooker Championship?

12. Which team won the last FA Cup final at the old Wembley and the first at the new Wembley?

13. Which Formula One Grand Prix took place at Hockenheimring?

14. The Rowley Mile is a feature of which racecourse?

15. Which tennis player's name is an anagram of referred ogre?

16. Who is the BBC's horse racing correspondent?

17. What is the venue for the World Snooker Championship?

18. Who is the only English rugby union player to win 100 international Test caps?

19. What is the maximum number of players that an American football team can have on the pitch at any one time?
    a) 10
    b) 11
    c) 12

20. Which club's ground hosted football matches at the 2012 Olympics?
    a) Aston Villa
    b) Coventry City
    c) Wolverhampton Wanderers

Answers to Quiz 18: Horse Racing

1.	Epsom	11.	Kauto Star
2.	Lanfranco	12.	Don't Push It
3.	March	13.	Best Mate
4.	Paul Hanagan	14.	Ruby Walsh
5.	Robert Thornton	15.	Doncaster
6.	Paul Nicholls	16.	Neptune Collonges
7.	26 December	17.	Chepstow
8.	Synchronised	18.	Big Buck's
9.	Pour Moi	19.	30
10.	Sandown	20.	Tony McCoy

Quiz 20: Motorsport

1. Which Frenchman won the World Rally Championship Drivers' title every year from 2004 until 2011?

2. What does the TT in the Isle of Man TT stand for?

3. What nationality is the Formula One driver Sébastian Buemi?

4. In the 2012 Formula One season, how many points were awarded for a second place finish?

5. What is the name of Peterborough's Elite League speedway team?

6. Which manufacturer was the sole tyre provider during the 2012 Formula One season?

7. Who won seven Moto GP championships between 2001 and 2009?

8. Which team won the 2011 Elite League Speedway Championship?

9. Which American won the 2011 Speedway Grand Prix final?

10. Which country has provided the most Formula One World Champions?

11. Which Spaniard won the 500cc Moto GP Riders' Championship in 2010?

12. At what circuit did the 2012 British Moto GP take place?

13. What nationality is Moto GP rider Casey Stoner?

14. What three races make up the so-called Triple Crown of Motorsport?

15. Which British driver is the only man to complete the Triple Crown?

16. The Aces is the nickname of which Elite League speedway team?

17. Which circuit hosted the British Moto GP from 1987 until 2009?

18. Who was the only Finnish driver to race in the 2011 Formula One season?

19. Which Formula One team has won the most Constructors' titles?
    a) Ferrari
    b) McLaren
    c) Williams

20. What did Beatles fan Sebastian Vettel name his 2012 F1 car?
    a) Abbey
    b) Eleanor
    c) Jude

Answers to Quiz 19: Pot Luck

1. Nigel Mansell
2. January
3. 12
4. Wales
5. 4
6. Catalan Dragons and Paris St Germain
7. Carlos Tevez
8. Arthur Ashe
9. Kevin Sinfield
10. Gavin Henson
11. Ronnie O'Sullivan and Stephen Hendry
12. Chelsea
13. The German Grand Prix
14. Newmarket
15. Roger Federer
16. Cornelius Lysaght
17. The Crucible Theatre
18. Jason Leonard
19. 11
20. Coventry City

Quiz 21: Pot Luck

1. Which two teams are Italy yet to beat in rugby union's Six Nations Championship?

2. Which Australian footballer is married to former Emmerdale actress Sheree Murphy?

3. Easter Road is the home ground of which Scottish football team?

4. Amen Corner is a trio of holes at which golf course?

5. Sir Alex Ferguson joined Manchester United from which club?

6. The Clones Cyclone was the nickname of which Irish boxer?

7. In which South American city is the Maracanã Stadium?

8. Which country lost in the World Cup final in 1982 and 1986?

9. Who did David Moyes succeed as manager of Everton?

10. Over what distance is the marathon run?

11. Which rugby union team play their home games at The Rec?

12. Who were Chelsea's two goal scorers in the 2012 FA Cup final?

13. Which four sports make up the Olympic aquatics programme?

14. The Rocket is the nickname of which snooker player?

15. Who were the first London club to win the Champions League?

16. What are the five events that make up a modern pentathlon?

17. Valley Parade is the home ground of which English football club?

18. What is the only Caribbean country to host the Commonwealth Games?

19. Jockey Tony McCoy is a huge fan of which football club?
    a) Arsenal
    b) Liverpool
    c) Manchester United

20. Who is the only driver during a single season to have a podium finish in every Formula One race that he started?
    a) Michael Schumacher
    b) Ayrton Senna
    c) Sebastian Vettel

Answers to Quiz 20: Motorsport

1. Sébastien Loeb
2. Tourist Trophy
3. Swiss
4. 18
5. Panthers
6. Pirelli
7. Valentino Rossi
8. Poole Pirates
9. Greg Hancock
10. United Kingdom
11. Jorge Lorenzo
12. Silverstone
13. Australian
14. Monaco Grand Prix, 24 Hours of Le Mans and the Indianapolis 500
15. Graham Hill
16. Belle Vue
17. Donington Park
18. Heiki Kovalainen
19. Ferrari
20. Abbey

Quiz 22: Olympic Games

1. In what year did the first Modern Olympics take place?

2. Who was disqualified after winning the men's 100m at the 1988 Games?

3. How many rings are on the Olympic flag?

4. What were names of the mascots of the 2012 London Games?

5. Which British sailor won silver at the 1996 Games and then gold in 2000, 2004 and 2008?

6. Which two martial arts featured at the 2012 Olympic Games?

7. Christine Ohuruogu won gold at the 2008 Games in which track event?

8. Greco-Romano and Freestyle are styles of which sport?

9. Which 2012 Olympic event took place at Horse Guards Parade?

10. Kelly Holmes won double Olympic gold in 2004 at which two athletic events?

11. Which South American city will host the 2016 Olympic Games?

12. In what year did Linford Christie win the 100m gold medal?

13. Who won Britain's first swimming gold medal since 1988 at the 2008 Beijing Games?

14. Which American swimmer won eight gold medals in 2008?

15. Which brothers won gold for Britain in the rowing coxed pairs at Barcelona in 1992?

16. Which Australian, who won five gold medals in the pool in 2000 and 2004, failed in his attempt to qualify for the 2012 Games?

17. Prior to Usain Bolt in 2008, who was the last man to complete the 100m and 200m double?

18. What are the three Asian cities to have hosted the Summer Olympic Games?

19. How long is an Olympic table tennis table?
    a) 8 feet
    b) 9 feet
    c) 10 feet

20. Which of the following is not an Olympic sport?
    a) badminton
    b) squash
    c) tennis

Answers to Quiz 21: Pot Luck

1. England and Ireland
2. Harry Kewell
3. Hibernian
4. Augusta National
5. Aberdeen
6. Barry McGuigan
7. Rio de Janeiro
8. West Germany
9. Walter Smith
10. 26 miles 385 yards
11. Bath
12. Ramires and Drogba
13. Swimming, diving, synchronised swimming and water polo
14. Ronnie O'Sullivan
15. Chelsea
16. Shooting, swimming, fencing, running and horse riding
17. Bradford City
18. Jamaica
19. Arsenal
20. Michael Schumacher

Quiz 23: Pot Luck

1. What is the only country to lose three Rugby World Cup finals?

2. In betting, what odds are represented by Burlington Bertie?

3. Who won the pole vault gold medal in the first six World Athletics Championships?

4. Who were the first British club to win a major European football trophy?

5. Which Manchester United pair were suspended from the 1999 Champions League final?

6. Matt Biondi won 8 Olympic medals between 1984 and 1992 in which sport?

7. What are the four teams in American football's NFL whose name starts with the letter C?

8. What nationality is Manchester City full back Pablo Zabaleta?

9. Who is Scotland's most capped footballer?

10. Which country won cricket's first World Twenty20 competition in 2007?

11. Alastair Cook plays domestic cricket for which English county?

12. In what year did England reach the final of the Rugby World Cup for the first time?

13. Who did Giovanni Trapattoni succeed as permanent manager of the Republic of Ireland?

14. Which country won the gold medal in rugby 7s at the Commonwealth Games in 1998, 2002, 2006 and 2010?

15. What colour jersey is worn by the overall race leader in cycling's Tour de France?

16. Which Irishman has made the most appearances in the history of rugby union's Heineken Cup?

17. The Coventry Bees and Swindon Robins are teams in which sport?

18. Who are the only team to go through an entire Premier League season without losing a match?

19. How old was Boris Becker when he won his first Wimbledon Men's Singles title?
    a) 16
    b) 17
    c) 18

20. What is the venue for the Super League Grand Final?
    a) Old Trafford
    b) Twickenham
    c) Wembley

Answers to Quiz 22: Olympic Games

1. 1896	11. Rio de Janeiro
2. Ben Johnson	12. 1992
3. Five	13. Rebecca Adlington
4. Wenlock and Mandeville	14. Michael Phelps
5. Ben Ainslie	15. Greg and Jonny Searle
6. Judo and taekwondo	16. Ian Thorpe
7. 400m	17. Carl Lewis in 1984
8. Wrestling	18. Tokyo, Seoul and Beijing
9. Beach volleyball	19. 9 feet
10. 800m and 1500m	20. Squash

Quiz 24: Rugby League

1. Which haulage firm is the sponsor of the Super League?

2. The Halliwell Jones Stadium is the home ground of which team?

3. Which team did Catalan Dragons beat 76-6 in March 2012?

4. The Airlie Birds is the nickname of which team?

5. Who won the Man of Steel award in 2011?

6. Which team has won the most Challenge Cup finals?

7. Who has played rugby league for Great Britain and rugby union for Ireland?

8. Which team won the 2011 Super League Grand Final?

9. Who did they beat in the final?

10. Which player holds the record for the most appearances in the Challenge Cup final?

11. Which Aussie legend hung up his boots in 2011, missing a kick in front of the posts in the 4 Nations final with his last action?

12. Who has kicked the most goals in the Super League era?

13. Beep Beep is the nickname of which Leeds Rhino?

14. Which Wigan forward won the Lance Todd trophy in 2011?

15. Which two Super League clubs were deducted points for entering administration during the 2011 season?

16. Who did Leeds beat to win the 2012 World Club Challenge?

17. Who did St Helens defeat in the 2006 Super League Grand Final?

EASY

18. Which Aussie was appointed coach of Bradford Bulls in 2011?

19. In what year did Hull KR meet Hull FC in the Challenge Cup Final?
    a) 1980
    b) 1985
    c) 1990

20. How many teams compete in the Super League?
    a) 10
    b) 12
    c) 14

Answers to Quiz 23: Pot Luck

1. France
2. 100/30
3. Sergey Bubka
4. Tottenham Hotspur
5. Roy Keane and Paul Scholes
6. Swimming
7. Carolina Panthers, Chicago Bears, Cincinnati Bengals, Cleveland Browns
8. Argentine
9. Kenny Dalglish
10. India
11. Essex
12. 1991
13. Steve Staunton
14. New Zealand
15. Yellow
16. Ronan O'Gara
17. Speedway
18. Arsenal
19. 17
20. Old Trafford

Quiz 25: Pot Luck

1. Who is the youngest winner of the Men's Singles title at Wimbledon?

2. What size is a full-size snooker table?

3. Over what distance is the Grand National run?

4. Who is the only left-handed golfer to have won the US PGA?

5. Which Irishman made 722 appearances for Arsenal between 1975 and 1993?

6. Who succeeded Martin Johnson as coach of the England rugby union team?

7. Who is the Republic of Ireland's all-time leading goal scorer?

8. What are the seven English clubs to have reached the final of the European Cup / Champions League?

9. Keiron Cunningham spent the whole of his career with which rugby league club?

10. In what sport do teams compete for the America's Cup?

11. Who was appointed manager of the Wales national football team in 2012?

12. Who was the last Australian to win the Men's Singles at Wimbledon?

13. How long in yards is a cricket pitch?

14. The film Million Dollar Baby is about which sport?

15. Peeves Inner Kit is an anagram of which England cricketer?

16. How many teams took part in rugby union's Aviva Premiership in 2011/12?

17. What trophy is awarded to the winner of rugby matches between England and Scotland?

18. Who is the only Englishman to be named International Rugby Board Player of the Year?

19. Who was the first footballer to win 100 international caps for England?
    a) Bobby Charlton
    b) Bobby Moore
    c) Billy Wright

20. What are National Hunt flat races also known as?
    a) bashers
    b) boxers
    c) bumpers

Answers to Quiz 24: Rugby League

1. Eddie Stobart
2. Warrington Wolves
3. Widnes
4. Hull FC
5. Rangi Chase
6. Wigan
7. Brian Carney
8. Leeds
9. St Helens
10. Shaun Edwards
11. Darren Lockyer
12. Kevin Sinfield
13. Rob Burrow
14. Jeff Lima
15. Crusaders and Wakefield
16. Manly-Warringah Sea Eagles
17. Hull FC
18. Mick Potter
19. 1980
20. 14

Quiz 26: Rugby Union

1. Which country won the 2011 Rugby World Cup?

2. What is the name of the trophy given to the winners of the Rugby World Cup?

3. Who was appointed coach of the Scotland rugby team in 2009?

4. Which Welshman was controversially sent off in the 2011 World Cup semi-final?

5. Which two teams competed in the final of the 2012 Heineken Cup?

6. Who is Scotland's all-time record international points scorer?

7. Sixways is the home of which English rugby club?

8. Which two international teams compete for the Cook Cup?

9. Who knocked England and Wales out of the 2011 Rugby World Cup?

10. Who has scored the most international tries for Wales?

11. Who is the most capped player in international rugby history?

12. In 2009, Jonny Wilkinson joined which French club?

13. Who are the two Welshmen to have scored over 250 points in the Six Nations Championship?

14. Can you name the four English sides to have won the Heineken Cup?

15. Where do the Leicester Tigers play their home games?

16. Israel Dagg plays international rugby for which country?

Answers - page 55

17. How many times have Ireland completed a Six Nations Grand Slam?

18. Who scored England's only try in their 2003 World Cup final victory over Australia?

19. In 2013, the British and Irish Lions will tour which country?
    a) Australia
    b) New Zealand
    c) South Africa

20. In what country was Ronan O'Gara born?
    a) England
    b) Ireland
    c) USA

EASY

Answers to Quiz 25: Pot Luck

1. Boris Becker
2. 12 feet by 6 feet
3. 4 miles 4 furlongs
4. Phil Mickelson
5. David O'Leary
6. Stuart Lancaster
7. Robbie Keane
8. Manchester United, Liverpool, Nottingham Forest, Aston Villa, Chelsea, Leeds United and Arsenal
9. St Helens
10. Yachting
11. Chris Coleman
12. Lleyton Hewitt
13. 22 yards
14. Boxing
15. Kevin Pietersen
16. 12
17. Calcutta Cup
18. Johnny Wilkinson
19. Billy Wright
20. Bumpers

Quiz 27: Pot Luck

1. Which city will host the 2014 Commonwealth Games?

2. What nationality is tennis player Caroline Wozniacki?

3. Who was the National Hunt Champion Trainer for ten successive seasons between 1995 and 2005?

4. Which England rugby union player is noted for his 'swallow dive' celebrations?

5. Which dart player goes by the nickname The Wizard?

6. Which South African coached the Italian rugby union team from 2007 until 2011?

7. At the start of a frame of snooker, how many balls are on the table?

8. Who is the youngest footballer to score an international goal for England?

9. Newton Heath was the original name of which football club?

10. Who in 2011 became the first Chinese player to win a tennis grand slam event?

11. Who was the coach of the New Zealand All Blacks at the 2011 Rugby World Cup?

12. Fiba is the world governing body of which sport?

13. Who captained the British and Irish Lions on their tours to South Africa in 1997 and Australia in 2001?

14. What town is home to a rugby league team called the Tigers?

15. Who is the most capped Welsh footballer?

16. After leaving Wigan Warriors, Andy Farrell joined which rugby union club?

17. Which former Manchester United player steered Molde to their first ever Norwegian title in 2011?

18. Which snooker player is known as The Wizard of Wishaw?

19. Who is the only player in his forties to score in the Premier League?

20. Only one Rugby World Cup final has featured two teams from the Southern hemisphere. In what year did it take place?
    a) 1987
    b) 1991
    c) 1995

21. Who is Arsenal's all-time leading goal scorer?
    a) Thierry Henry
    b) Robin van Persie
    c) Ian Wright

Answers to Quiz 26: Rugby Union

1. New Zealand
2. Webb-Ellis Trophy
3. Andy Robinson
4. Sam Warburton
5. Leinster and Ulster
6. Chris Paterson
7. Worcester Warriors
8. England and Australia
9. France
10. Shane Williams
11. George Gregan
12. Toulon
13. Neil Jenkins and Stephen Jones
14. Bath, Northampton, Leicester and Wasps
15. Welford Road
16. New Zealand
17. Twice
18. Jason Robinson
19. Australia
20. USA

Quiz 28: Snooker

1. Who won the 2012 World Snooker Championship?

2. The Whirlwind is the nickname of which snooker player?

3. Who was the first Australian to win the World Championship?

4. Which 52-year-old shocked John Higgins in the 2010 World Championship?

5. Who was the first player to hit a maximum break at the World Championship?

6. Who hit a 147 in the 2012 World Championship?

7. Which 150/1 outsider won the World Championship in 2005?

8. Who is the only left-handed player to have won the World Championship?

9. Who holds the record for the most ranking tournament victories?

10. Which bookmaker was the sponsor of the 2012 World Championship?

11. Who is the youngest player to qualify for the World Snooker Championship?

12. How many World Championships did Steve Davis win?

13. Who won the World Championship in 1972 and 1982?

14. Which two snooker players have appeared on Strictly Come Dancing?

15. Can you name the three Welshmen to have won the World Championship?

16. Who is the only player from the Republic of Ireland to win the World Championship?

17. How many balls must a player pot to make a maximum 147 break?
    a) 34
    b) 36
    c) 38

18. John Higgins is a fan of which football club?
    a) Aberdeen
    b) Celtic
    c) Rangers

19. Who came back from an 8-0 deficit to win the 1985 World Championship final?

20. Prolific potter Tony Drago is from which country?

Answers to Quiz 27: Pot Luck

1. Glasgow
2. Danish
3. Martin Pipe
4. Chris Ashton
5. Simon Whitlock
6. Nick Mallett
7. 22
8. Wayne Rooney
9. Manchester United
10. Li Na in the French Open
11. Graham Henry
12. Basketball
13. Martin Johnson
14. Castleford
15. Neville Southall
16. Saracens
17. Ole Gunnar Solskjaer
18. John Higgins
19. Teddy Sheringham
20. 1995
21. Thierry Henry

Quiz 29: Pot Luck

1. Which player made 8 Premier League appearances in 2011/12, was sent off in two and scored in the other six?

2. Which football team beat Blackpool in the 2011/12 Championship play-off final?

3. Which Irish province plays home rugby matches at Ravenhill Stadium?

4. In rugby league, what number shirt does a hooker wear?

5. And what number shirt does the hooker wear in rugby union?

6. New Road is the home ground of which county cricket team?

7. The owners of Liverpool Football Club are also the owners of which baseball team?

8. What is the only team that plays in cricket's County Championship whose name starts with a vowel?

9. Who won the Masters Snooker in 2012?

10. Which Formula One Grand Prix is hosted at the Circuit de Catalunya circuit?

11. Who did Manchester United beat in the 2010 League Cup final?

12. Who are the two Swedes to have won the Men's Singles at Wimbledon?

13. Who are the four football clubs to have won England's top flight whose name starts with a vowel?

14. Which Australian completed the tennis grand slam in 1962 and 1969?

15. At which racecourse is the King George VI Chase run?

16. Denise Lewis won Olympic gold in which event?

17. How high is a tennis net at its centre?

18. Which Russian won the Australian Open Men's Singles in 2005?

19. Fast bowler James Anderson plays domestic cricket for which English county?
    a) Lancashire
    b) Warwickshire
    c) Yorkshire

20. In which American state is the Pebble Beach golf course?
    a) California
    b) Florida
    c) New York

Answers to Quiz 28: Snooker

1. Ronnie O'Sullivan
2. Jimmy White
3. Neal Robertson
4. Steve Davis
5. Cliff Thorburn
6. Stephen Hendry
7. Shaun Murphy
8. Mark Williams
9. Stephen Hendry
10. Betfred
11. Luca Brecel
12. Six
13. Alex Higgins
14. Willie Thorne and Dennis Taylor
15. Ray Reardon, Terry Griffiths and Mark Williams
16. Ken Doherty
17. 36
18. Celtic
19. Dennis Taylor
20. Malta

Quiz 30: Tennis

EASY

1. Who won the 2011 Men's Singles at Wimbledon?

2. Who did he beat in the final?

3. The French Open is hosted at a stadium named after which WWI pilot?

4. What is the last Grand Slam tournament of the year?

5. Who holds the record for the most Wimbledon Ladies' Singles Championship titles?

6. Andy Murray lost his first two Grand Slam finals to which opponent?

7. Who came from two sets to love down to beat Roger Federer in the quarter-finals at Wimbledon in 2011?

8. What is the female equivalent of the Davis Cup?

9. Who was the last English player to win the Men's Singles at Wimbledon?

10. What is the only Grand Slam tournament played on clay?

11. Who are the two unseeded players to have won the Men's Singles at Wimbledon?

12. Deliciano is the nickname of which Spanish player?

13. Which major was held on grass for the last time in 1987?

14. Who has won the most Grand Slam titles in the history of men's tennis?

15. How many Wimbledon Men's Singles titles did Björn Borg win?

16. What nationality is 2011 Wimbledon Ladies' Singles champion Petra Kvitova?

EASY

17. Who was the first Russian woman to win the Ladies' Singles at Wimbledon?

18. Who was appointed Andy Murray's coach in 2011?

19. How many players take part in the Men's Singles at Wimbledon?
    a) 128
    b) 148
    c) 168

20. Prior to Andy Murray, who was the last Briton to reach a Grand Slam final?
    a) Tim Henman
    b) John Lloyd
    c) Greg Rusedski

Answers to Quiz 29: Pot Luck

1. Djibril Cisse
2. West Ham United
3. Ulster
4. 9
5. 2
6. Worcestershire
7. Boston Red Sox
8. Essex
9. Neal Robertson
10. Spanish
11. Aston Villa
12. Björn Borg and Stefan Edberg
13. Arsenal, Aston Villa, Everton and Ipswich Town
14. Rod Laver
15. Kempton Park
16. Heptathlon
17. 3ft
18. Marat Safin
19. Lancashire
20. California

Quiz 31: Pot Luck

1. Which player has made the most appearances in the Rugby World Cup?

2. The Hammer is the nickname of which dart player?

3. Who is the only Welsh golfer to win a major?

4. What were the two countries at Euro 2012 that started with the letter R?

5. Griffin Park is the home ground of which London football club?

6. What sport was the subject of the film Any Given Sunday?

7. Manchester United completed their famous 1999 treble by beating which team in the Champions League final?

8. What name is shared by a prolific English goal scorer and Wales' 2005 Grand Slam winning captain?

9. Who resigned as manager of Aston Villa just days before the start of the 2010/11 season?

10. Who scored Manchester United's two last gasp goals in the 1999 Champions League final?

11. TalkSport host Ronnie Irani played cricket for which two English counties?

12. Who was the last player to win the Men's Singles at Wimbledon whose surname starts with a vowel?

13. Who was the non-playing captain of Europe's triumphant 2010 Ryder Cup team?

14. Lambeau Field is the home stadium of which NFL team?

15. Who did Paul Lambert succeed as manager of Norwich City?

16. Who was the manager of the Spain team that won the 2010 World Cup?

17. Which country will host the 2018 World Cup?

18. What is the name of Gloucester RFC's home ground?

19. The 1977 film comedy Slap Shot is about which sport?
    a) American football
    b) basketball
    c) ice hockey

20. In golf's Ryder Cup, each team contains how many players?
    a) 10
    b) 11
    c) 12

Answers to Quiz 30: Tennis

1. Novak Djokovic
2. Rafael Nadal
3. Roland Garros
4. US Open
5. Martina Navratilova
6. Roger Federer
7. Jo-Wilfried Tsonga
8. The Fed Cup (formerly The Federation Cup)
9. Fred Perry
10. The French Open
11. Boris Becker and Goran Ivanišević
12. Feliciano López
13. Australian Open
14. Roger Federer
15. 5
16. Czech
17. Maria Sharapova
18. Ivan Lendl
19. 128
20. Greg Rusedski

Quiz 32: US Sports

EASY

1. Tom Brady is the long-time quarterback of which NFL team?

2. Fenway Park is the home ground of which baseball team?

3. In which American city do the NBA's Pistons play?

4. Which baseball team has won the World Series the most times?

5. British basketball star Luol Deng plays for which American team?

6. Which NFL team won the first Super Bowl?

7. The only Major League Baseball team in Canada is based in which city?

8. Which team has won the Super Bowl the most times?

9. After 13 seasons with the Indianapolis Colts, quarterback Peyton Manning joined which team in 2012?

10. Which team won the Stanley Cup in 2011?

11. What is the name of the the trophy awarded to the winner of the Super Bowl?

12. The Penguins are an ice hockey team in which American city?

13. What award is given to the best defensive performer at each position in Major League Baseball?

14. Who traditionally throws the ceremonial first pitch of the baseball season?

15. In which American city will you find professional sports teams called Broncos, Nuggets and Rockies?

16. Which NFL team calls Soldier Field home?

17. Joe Montana and Steve Young won the Super Bowl with which team?

18. Which team won the MLS championship in 2011?

19. Which quarterback has steered the New York Giants to two Super Bowl victories?
    a) Archie Manning
    b) Eli Manning
    c) Peyton Manning

20. How many teams are in the NFL?
    a) 28
    b) 30
    c) 32

Answers to Quiz 31: Pot Luck

1. Jason Leonard
2. Andy Hamilton
3. Ian Woosnam
4. Russia and Republic of Ireland
5. Brentford
6. American football
7. Bayern Munich
8. Michael Owen
9. Martin O'Neill
10. Teddy Sheringham and Ole Gunnar Solskjaer
11. Lancashire and Essex
12. Goran Ivanišević
13. Colin Montgomerie
14. Green Bay Packers
15. Bryan Gunn
16. Vicente del Bosque
17. Russia
18. Kingsholm
19. Ice hockey
20. 12

Quiz 33: Pot Luck

EASY

1. Which city hosted the 2010 Commonwealth Games?

2. Striker Mario Gómez plays international football for which country?

3. The Vetch Field was the former ground of which football club?

4. What is the female equivalent of the Ryder Cup?

5. The Eredivisie is the top-flight football competition in which country?

6. Wantage Road is the home ground of which county cricket team?

7. Which British athlete set the world record for the triple jump at the 1995 World Championships?

8. What nationality is the golfer Vijay Singh?

9. What is the second largest stadium in the British Isles?

10. Who scored Chelsea's 88th minute equaliser in the 2012 Champions League final?

11. Which rugby union team play their home games at Reading's Madejski Stadium?

12. What is the South American equivalent of the UEFA Champions League?

13. Who won the women's wheelchair race at the London Marathon six times between 1992 and 2002?

14. Tannadice Park is the home ground of which Scottish football club?

15. The Canal Turn and Valentine's Brook are features of which racecourse?

16. Which country eliminated England from Euro 2004 and the 2006 World Cup?

17. Who was the last English woman to win the Ladies' Singles at Wimbledon?

18. Who is older, Serena or Venus Williams?

19. Which Caribbean country made its debut at the 2006 World Cup?
    a) Barbados
    b) Jamaica
    c) Trinidad and Tobago

20. In what year did Scotland last qualify for the World Cup?
    a) 1994
    b) 1998
    c) 2002

Answers to Quiz 32: US Sports

1. New England Patriots
2. Boston Red Sox
3. Detroit
4. New York Yankees
5. Chicago Bulls
6. Green Bay Packers
7. Toronto
8. Pittsburgh Steelers
9. Denver Broncos
10. Boston Bruins
11. The Vince Lombardi Trophy
12. Pittsburgh
13. A Gold Glove
14. The President of the USA
15. Denver
16. Chicago Bears
17. San Francisco 49ers
18. LA Galaxy
19. Eli Manning
20. 32

MEDIUM QUIZZES

Quiz 34: Pot Luck

1. Shanaze Reade is a world champion in which sport?

2. Who did Harry Redknapp succeed as manager of Tottenham?

3. In a greyhound race, the dog in which trap wears a black and white striped jacket?

4. Which football team dropped down into the third tier of English football for the first time in 48 years in 2012?

5. Which England rugby player was banned for five weeks in 2011 after punching Chris Ashton?

6. Which amateur jockey rode the winner in the 2011 Cheltenham Gold Cup?

7. Which horse did he steer to victory?

8. The Raging Potato is the nickname of which Irish rugby player?

9. What nationality are tennis players Kim Clijsters and Justine Henin?

10. What was the first city outside Europe to host the Summer Olympics?

11. In addition to Jamaica, sprinter Merlene Ottey also represented which country?

12. What are the four teams that have spent a single season in the Premier League?

13. Which all-rounder captained the West Indies on their 2012 tour of England?

14. Andy Jameson was a British Olympic medallist in which sport?

15. What is the opening event of the second day of an Olympic decathlon?

16. Ricky Hatton won world titles in which two weight divisions?

17. The first ever cricket Test match was held at which ground?

18. Who were the original team captains on A Question of Sport?

19. What nationality is the World Champion sprint hurdler Sally Pearson?
    a) American
    b) Australian
    c) Jamaican

20. How many teams took part in the 2011 Rugby World Cup?
    a) 16
    b) 18
    c) 20

Answers to Quiz 67: Firsts and Lasts

1. 1975
2. Both boats sank
3. Brazil in 1994
4. Complete the Grand National
5. 1950
6. Sir Richard Hadlee
7. Villa Park
8. Jesper Blomqvist
9. Birmingham City
10. Roger Federer
11. Allan Clarke in 1970
12. Mary Pierce
13. Arsenal
14. USSR
15. The University Boat Race
16. 1992
17. Eden Gardens, Calcutta
18. Graham Onions
19. 1967
20. 1986

Quiz 35: Athletics

1. Which Asian city hosted the 2011 World Athletics Championship?

2. Which athlete won the men's 1500m title at the 1997, 1999, 2001 and 2003 World Championships?

3. Who won nine consecutive heptathlon golds in major championships in the 2000s?

4. Which Frenchwoman was the first woman to win the 400m at two consecutive Olympics?

5. What nationality is decathlon world record holder Roman Šebrle?

6. Which sprinter won medals in the 100m at both the 2003 and the 2011 World Championships?

7. Who were the two British female athletes to win a medal at the 2011 World Athletics Championships?

8. What is the eighth event of an Olympic decathlon?

9. The American-born Tiffany Ofili-Porter is the British record holder at which event?

10. Who won the women's pole vault World Championship in 2004, 2006, 2008 and 2012?

11. In what English city do The Great City Games take place?

12. Holly Bleasdale is a British record holder in which event?

13. Who won the IAAF World Female Athlete of the Year in 2002?

14. Which British-born athlete won two World Athletics Championship long jump golds for Italy?

15. The British record time of 19.94s for the 200m was set in 1993 by which athlete?

16. Usain Bolt ran the 100m at the 2009 World Championships in Berlin in what time?

17. Mo Farah set the British record at 5,000m in 2010. Whose time did he beat to set that record?
    a) Eamon Martin
    b) David Moorcroft
    c) Mark Rowland

18. In what year did the first World Athletics Championships take place?
    a) 1981
    b) 1983
    c) 1985

19. Which British athlete won gold in the men's 400m hurdles at the 2012 European Championships?

20. Who won silver in the women's 10,000m at the 2012 European Championships?

MEDIUM

Answers to Quiz 34: Pot Luck

1. BMX
2. Juande Ramos
3. Trap 6
4. Coventry City
5. Manu Tuilagi
6. Sam Waley-Cohen
7. Long Run
8. Keith Wood
9. Belgian
10. St Louis
11. Slovenia
12. Blackpool, Barnsley, Burnley and Swindon Town
13. Darren Sammy
14. Swimming
15. 110m hurdles
16. Light welterweight and welterweight
17. The Melbourne Cricket Ground
18. Henry Cooper and Cliff Morgan
19. Australian
20. 20

Quiz 36: Pot Luck

1. What is the only horse to have won the King George VI Chase five times?

2. Which Harlequins winger received a ban for his part in the so-called 'Bloodgate' fake injury scandal?

3. Who were the three players to score ten or more goals in the 2011/12 Champions League?

4. Which Welsh rugby player was stopped by police driving a golf buggy on a motorway after a Six Nations victory in 2010?

5. Which club received the most yellow cards in the 2011/12 Champions League?

6. What is the only Romanian club to win the European Cup?

7. What was the last team other than Celtic or Rangers to win the Scottish Premier League?

8. The British record time of 3:29.67 for the men's 1,500m was set in 1985 by which athlete?

9. How many players are on a volleyball team?

10. Who are the two World Cup winners to have managed Chelsea?

11. Kevin Pietersen has played English domestic cricket for which three counties?

12. Which Frenchman was the coach of rugby union's Sale Sharks from 2004 to 2009?

13. Sean Kerly was a prolific scorer for Great Britain in which sport?

14. Which two players captained the England team during their ill-fated 2011 Rugby World Cup campaign?

15. Who was England's first openly gay cricketer?

16. Errands twas us is an anagram of which cricketer?

17. In which Spanish city are football club Espanyol based?

18. Who scored the winning drop goal to give South Africa victory over New Zealand in the 1995 Rugby World Cup final?

19. Adrian Moorhouse, David Wilkie and Duncan Goodhew won Olympic swimming gold medals at which stroke?
    a) backstroke
    b) breaststroke
    c) butterfly

20. What height is the platform in Olympic diving events?
    a) 8m
    b) 9m
    c) 10m

Answers to Quiz 35: Athletics

1. Daegu
2. Hicham El Guerrouj
3. Carolina Klüft
4. Marie-José Pérec
5. Czech
6. Kim Collins
7. Hannah England and Jessica Ennis
8. Pole vault
9. 110m hurdles
10. Yelena Isinbayeva
11. Manchester
12. Pole vault
13. Paula Radcliffe
14. Fiona May
15. John Regis
16. 9.59 seconds
17. David Moorcroft
18. 1983
19. Rhys Williams
20. Jo Pavey

MEDIUM

Quiz 37: The A Team

MEDIUM

1. Who took 405 wickets in 98 Test matches for the West Indies?

2. Which much decorated England footballer was manager of Wycombe Wanderers in 2003/04?

3. The Angels are a baseball team based in which American city?

4. Who scored 396 points for the England rugby union team between 1985 and 1997?

5. What event was hosted at Lord's cricket ground at the 2012 Olympics?

6. Who was the leading wicket taker in the Ashes series of 1981?

7. Dial Square was the original name of which football club?

8. Which batsman was run out on 99 in the 1993 Ashes Test at Lord's?

9. Which sprinter finished fifth in the 100m at the 2004 and 2008 Olympics?

10. Who was the first cyclist to win the Tour de France five times?

11. Who is the only Austrian footballer with a Premier League winner's medal?

12. What is the name of Bristol City's home ground?

13. Who is the only Scotsman to have played football for Barcelona?

14. El Nano is the nickname of which Formula One driver?

15. Which seam bowler played nine One Day Internationals for England in 1998 and 1999?

16. Which four members of England's Euro 2012 squad have a first name beginning with A?

17. Which Trinidadian sprinter won four medals in the 100m and 200m at the 1996 and 2000 Olympics?

18. Which country finished in third place at the 2007 Rugby World Cup?

19. What is the name of Melbourne's Formula One circuit?
    a) Albert Park
    b) Andrew Park
    c) Arthur Park

20. Somerset Park is the home ground of which Scottish football club?
    a) Aberdeen
    b) Arbroath
    c) Ayr United

MEDIUM

Answers to Quiz 36: Pot Luck

1. Kauto Star
2. Tom Williams
3. Lionel Messi, Mario Gómez and Cristiano Ronaldo
4. Andy Powell
5. Chelsea
6. Steaua Bucharest
7. Aberdeen
8. Steve Cram
9. 6
10. Sir Geoff Hurst and Luiz Felipe Scolari
11. Nottinghamshire, Hampshire and Surrey
12. Philippe Saint-André
13. Hockey
14. Lewis Moody and Mike Tindall
15. Steven Davies
16. Andrew Strauss
17. Barcelona
18. Joel Stransky
19. Breaststroke
20. 10m

Quiz 38: Pot Luck

1. The Cannibal was the nickname of which legendary cyclist?

2. In greyhound racing, what colour jacket is worn by the dog in trap one?

3. Who did Brendan Rodgers succeed as manager of Swansea City?

4. In what country was distance runner Mo Farah born?

5. In darts, what is the lowest score that cannot be finished with two darts?

6. Boyd Rankin plays international cricket for which country?

7. Who scored the only goal in the 2010 World Cup final?

8. True or false – no British city has ever hosted the European Athletics Championships?

9. Which Scottish football team play their home games at East End Park?

10. Which Australian took a hat-trick on his birthday during the 2010/11 Ashes series?

11. FINA is the world governing body for what sport?

12. In what sport could a participant perform a Lutz or an Axel?

13. What nationality is Formula One driver Sergio Pérez?

14. Which Wilmslow-born boxer won the Irish heavyweight title in 2012?

15. Who is the oldest player to win golf's US Masters?

16. Which city will host the 2017 World Athletics Championships?

17. Who played South African rugby captain Francois Pienaar in the 2009 film Invictus?

18. The Boulevard is the former ground of which rugby league team?

19. Who is the youngest England bowler to take 50 Test wickets?
    a) James Anderson
    b) Stuart Broad
    c) Steve Finn

20. Over how many innings is a baseball game usually played?
    a) 7
    b) 8
    c) 9

MEDIUM

Answers to Quiz 37: The A Team

1. Curtly Ambrose
2. Tony Adams
3. Anaheim
4. Rob Andrew
5. Archery
6. Terry Alderman
7. Arsenal
8. Michael Atherton
9. Asafa Powell
10. Jacques Anquetil
11. Alex Manninger
12. Ashton Gate
13. Steve Archibald
14. Fernando Alonso
15. Ian Austin
16. Ashley Cole, Ashley Young, Alex Oxlade-Chamberlain and Andy Carroll
17. Ato Boldon
18. Argentina
19. Albert Park
20. Ayr United

Quiz 39: Cricket

1. In which city will you find a cricket ground called the Kensington Oval?

2. Prior to Samit Patel, who was the last man to make his England Test debut?

3. Which Yorkshireman made his Test debut in England's 2012 Test against the West Indies at Lord's?

4. Who was the first batsman to score centuries in a Test match, an ODI and a Twenty20 international?

5. Which England bowler was appointed captain of Leicestershire in 2010?

6. Who has been on the losing side in the most Test matches?

7. In 2012, Shivnarine Chanderpaul set the record for the most Test appearances by a West Indian. Whose record did he break?

8. Who was the first Indian to score two Test match triple centuries?

9. Who took a hat-trick for England against the West Indies at Old Trafford in 1995?

10. Who was the first England spinner to take 50 Test wickets in a calendar year?

11. Who captained Lancashire to victory in the 2011 County Championship?

12. Which Indian was the first player to score centuries in every Test-playing nation?

13. Who was South Africa's first black captain?

14. Which England batsman made his Test debut in the 2005 Ashes series?

15. Who was the first England wicket-keeper to make a century on his Test debut?

16. Which Australian spinner took a wicket with his first ball in Test cricket against Sri Lanka in 2011?

17. Who are the three cricketers to have been permanent team captains on A Question of Sport?

18. Which Pakistani spinner bamboozled England by taking 24 wickets during their 3-0 Test series win over England in 2012?

19. In terms of Test match wins, who is Australia's most successful captain?
    a) Ricky Ponting
    b) Mark Taylor
    c) Steve Waugh

20. Which batsman smashed 128 from just 62 balls for Royal Challengers Bangalore in the IPL in 2012?
    a) Chris Gayle
    b) Matthew Hayden
    c) Virender Sehwag

MEDIUM

Answers to Quiz 38: Pot Luck

1. Eddy Merckx
2. Red
3. Paulo Sousa
4. Somalia
5. 99
6. Ireland
7. Andrés Iniesta
8. True
9. Dunfermline
10. Peter Siddle
11. Swimming (plus diving and water polo)
12. Figure skating
13. Mexican
14. Tyson Fury
15. Jack Nicklaus
16. London
17. Matt Damon
18. Hull FC
19. Steve Finn
20. 9

Quiz 40: Pot Luck

1. Which five sports have featured at every modern Olympic Games?

2. The fastest Test match half-century was scored in 2005 by which South African batsman?

3. What is the nickname of the New Zealand national football team?

4. What was the first horse to earn over £2m in prize money in jumps racing?

5. The Shrimps is the nickname of which Football League club?

6. What distance is the oche from a tournament dartboard?

7. In which American city are there professional sports teams called 76ers and Eagles?

8. The name of which British racecourse contains the fewest number of letters?

9. What was the first country to win the World Cup more than once?

10. Who is the only Canadian to win the Formula One World Drivers' Championship?

11. Who were the first two players to be sent off in an FA Cup final?

12. Which two rugby teams play for the James Bevan Trophy?

13. Which country has reached the most World Cup finals without winning the tournament?

14. What happened in Chelsea's game against Southampton on Boxing Day 1999 that had never previously occurred in English football?

15. Rabid dog ride is an anagram of which footballer?

16. Which country has qualified for the World Cup finals eight times but never passed the group stage?

17. Which West Indian bowler took a hat-trick at the 2011 Cricket World Cup?

18. Which two South American teams did England face at the 2006 World Cup?

19. Who won the BBC Sports Personality Team of the Year award in 2009 and 2011?

20. Which legendary boxer did not win an Olympic gold medal?
    a) Oscar de la Hoya
    b) Roy Jones Jr
    c) Sugar Ray Leonard

MEDIUM

Answers to Quiz 39: Cricket

1. Bridgetown, Barbados
2. Ajmal Shahzad
3. Jonny Bairstow
4. Chris Gayle
5. Matthew Hoggard
6. Shivnarine Chanderpaul
7. Courtney Walsh
8. Virender Sehwag
9. Dominic Cork
10. Graeme Swann
11. Glen Chapple
12. Rahul Dravid
13. Ashwell Prince
14. Kevin Pietersen
15. Matt Prior
16. Nathan Lyon
17. Fred Trueman, Sir Ian Botham and Phil Tufnell
18. Saeed Ajmal
19. Ricky Ponting
20. Chris Gayle

Quiz 41: Cycling

MEDIUM

1. Five riders have won the Tour de France five times or more. Can you name them?

2. Who beat Mark Cavendish to the Green Jersey by just 9 points in the 2010 Tour de France?

3. Who are the two riders to have won the Tour de France, Giro d'Italia and the World Road Race Championship in the same year?

4. Mark Cavendish left which team to join Team Sky?

5. Which Scot finished fourth overall and won the King of the Mountains competition in the 1984 Tour de France?

6. What colour jersey is worn by the Best Young Rider at the Tour de France?

7. Who won the women's individual pursuit gold medal at the 2008 Olympic Games?

8. Which Norwegian won two stages of the 2011 Tour de France for Team Sky?

9. Who won Britain's first Olympic gold for 84 years at the 1992 Barcelona Games?

10. Who was the last Frenchman to win the Tour de France?

11. Mark Cavendish broke the record for the most Tour de France stage wins by a British rider in 2011. Whose record did he break?

12. Which former Tour de France stage winner is the Directeur Sportif for Team Sky?

13. Who won the 2012 Paris-Nice race?

14. Which American took part in his 16th Tour de France in 2011?

15. Who is the only Tour de France rider to win the King of the Mountains, the points and the overall title in the same year?

16. What colour jersey is worn by the leader of the Tour of Spain?

17. Who won the 2011 World Road Race Championship?

18. What name is given to the rider in last place of the Tour de France?

19. What is the narrowest margin of victory in the Tour de France?
    a) 8 seconds
    b) 18 seconds
    c) 28 seconds

20. In what year was the first Tour de France held?
    a) 1903
    b) 1913
    c) 1923

Answers to Quiz 40: Pot Luck

1. Athletics, cycling, fencing, gymnastics and swimming
2. Jacques Kallis
3. The All Whites
4. Kauto Star
5. Morecambe
6. 7ft 9 and 1/4in (2.37m)
7. Philadelphia
8. Ayr
9. Italy
10. Jacques Villeneuve
11. Kevin Moran and José Antonio Reyes
12. Australia and Wales
13. Holland
14. There wasn't a single English player in the Chelsea starting line-up
15. Didier Drogba
16. Scotland
17. Kemar Roach
18. Paraguay and Ecuador
19. The England cricket team
20. Roy Jones Jr

MEDIUM

Quiz 42: Pot Luck

1. Greg Hancock, Tomasz Gollob and Jason Crump are former World Champions in which sport?

2. What was the first city in the southern hemisphere to host the Summer Olympics?

3. Who captained the Spanish football team to victory in the 2010 World Cup?

4. Which wicket-keeper captained Nottinghamshire to cricket's County Championship in 2010?

5. Which two Chelsea players missed from the spot in their 2008 Champions League final penalty shoot-out?

6. In what year did Brazil win the World Cup for the first time?

7. Who won his only World Snooker Championship in 1986?

8. Which jockey won his first Derby on Never Say Die?

9. Mark Webber was one of two Australians to drive in the 2011 Formula One season. Who was the other?

10. Who were the runners-up in the first football World Cup final?

11. What number lies between 14 and 12 on a standard dartboard?

12. Which team that qualified for Euro 2012 last appeared in the finals of the European Championship in 1988?

13. Who was the first Australian to win the World Darts Championship?

14. Who were the two losing semi-finalists in Euro 2008?

15. What is the oldest of England's classic horse races?

16. Which Sri Lankan was the first player to take 4 wickets in 4 balls in an international match?

17. Who are the only parent and child to win the BBC Sports Personality of the Year award?

18. A piece of music called Drag Racer is the theme tune to which TV sport?

19. Which Irish province famously beat the New Zealand All Blacks in a 1978 tour match?
    a) Munster
    b) Leinster
    c) Ulster

20. Who are the three Dutch players to have won the World Darts Championship?

Answers to Quiz 41: Cycling

1. Lance Armstrong, Jacques Anquetil, Bernard Hinault, Eddy Merckx and Miguel Indurain
2. Alessandro Petacchi
3. Eddy Merckx and Stephen Roche
4. HTC-Highroad
5. Robert Millar
6. White
7. Rebecca Romero
8. Edvald Boasson Hagen
9. Chris Boardman
10. Bernard Hinault
11. Barry Hoban
12. Sean Yates
13. Bradley Wiggins
14. George Hincapie
15. Eddy Merckx
16. Red
17. Mark Cavendish
18. Lanterne rouge
19. 8 seconds
20. 1903

MEDIUM

Quiz 43: Darts

1. Which event is known as 'the FA Cup of darts' as there are no seeds and minnows can meet the top players?

2. Prior to taking up darts, which World Champion was an international javelin thrower?

3. Who are the two Scotsmen to have won the World Championship?

4. Which player walks on stage to One Step Beyond by Madness?

5. Who were the four wild card entrants in the 2012 Premier League competition?

6. Who won the Women's World Championship every year between 2001 and 2007?

7. Who did Phil Taylor beat to win his first world title?

8. Tony O'Shea is a fan of which football club?

9. The Tripod is the nickname of which player?

10. The 2010 and 2011 Winmau World Masters were held in which Yorkshire city?

11. Who sealed the 2000 BDO World Championship by hitting a 170 finish in the final leg?

12. Who lost three consecutive World Championship finals in 1989, 1990 and 1991?

13. Which player was known as Dreamboy during his years with the BDO?

14. Who was the first player from outside the UK to win the World Championship?

15. The record for the most 180s by a player at a single PDC World Championship is 60. Who set that record?

16. Who are the three players to have beaten Phil Taylor in a World Championship final?

17. Which player has appeared at the most BDO World Championships?

18. Who is the only player to have reached a BDO and PDC World Championship final but not won either?

19. England won the 2012 World Cup of Darts. Which country did they beat in the final?
    a) Australia
    b) Holland
    c) Scotland

20. Away from the oche, what was Co Stompe's occupation?
    a) bus driver
    b) taxi driver
    c) tram driver

Answers to Quiz 42: Pot Luck

1. Speedway
2. Melbourne
3. Iker Casillas
4. Chris Read
5. John Terry and Nicolas Anelka
6. 1958
7. Joe Johnson
8. Lester Piggott
9. Daniel Ricciardo
10. Argentina
11. 9
12. Republic of Ireland
13. Tony David
14. Russia and Turkey
15. The St Leger
16. Lasith Malinga
17. Princess Anne and Zara Phillips
18. Snooker
19. Munster
20. Raymond van Barneveld, Jelle Klaasen and Christian Kist

MEDIUM

Quiz 44: Pot Luck

1. The Kentucky Derby is run at which track?

2. Which boxer was nicknamed 'Hands of Stone'?

3. In a Formula One race, what colour flag warns a driver that he is about to be lapped?

4. I sojourn home is an anagram of which football manager?

5. Which jockey turned pundit won his only Grand National in 1996 on Rough Quest?

6. Brian Clough was in charge of which club prior to taking the manager's job at Leeds United?

7. Which Dutch player did Phil Taylor thrash 16-1 in the 2007 World Matchplay Darts?

8. Chemmy Alcott is a multiple British champion in which sport?

9. Which England defender was ruled out of Euro 2012 after fracturing his jaw in the final warm-up match?

10. In what year did all four home nations qualify for the World Cup?

11. Muhammad Ali's final professional fight was against which opponent?

12. Which two countries took part in the first ever rugby union international?

13. Which Premier League team drew 17 matches during the 2011/12 season?

14. Arrowhead is the home stadium of which NFL team?

15. Which Welshman holds the record for the longest penalty kick in international rugby union?

16. Which Swede was beaten in the final of the Men's Singles at the French Open in 2009 and 2010?

17. The Craven meeting is run at which racecourse?

18. The Borderers is the nickname of which Scottish Football League team?

19. Fabio Capello's last game in charge of England was a 1-0 win over which team?
    a) Holland
    b) Spain
    c) Sweden

20. Which British woman won the 1976 French Open tennis title?
    a) Sue Barker
    b) Ann Jones
    c) Virginia Wade

MEDIUM

Answers to Quiz 43: Darts

1. UK Open
2. Bob Anderson
3. Jocky Wilson and Les Wallace
4. Daryll Fitton
5. Simon Whitlock, Raymond van Barneveld, Andy Hamilton and Kevin Painter
6. Trina Gulliver
7. Eric Bristow
8. Stockport County
9. Roland Scholten
10. Hull
11. Ted Hankey
12. Eric Bristow
13. Gary Anderson
14. John Part
15. Adrian Lewis
16. Dennis Priestley, John Part and Raymond van Barneveld
17. Martin Adams
18. Simon Whitlock
19. Australia
20. Tram driver

Quiz 45: Football

1. Who was the first Italian player to collect a Premier League winner's medal?

2. Who was Scotland's manager the last time they qualified for the finals of a major tournament?

3. Which Euro 2012 manager is a guitarist in a rock band called Rawbau?

4. Which Premier League striker is the only player to play both football and hurling at Croke Park?

5. Prior to the 2011/12 season, when was the last time the top two teams in England's top flight finished with the same number of points?

6. Carlos Tevez was suspended by Manchester City after refusing to go on as a substitute in a Champions League game against which team?

7. Who are the three Scots to have won the Premier League Manager of the Year award?

8. Who are the only team to have played in the English top flight and not been relegated?

9. Which two teams met in the 2012 Scottish Cup final?

10. Which Premier League team recorded just seven wins in 2011/12, their worst total since 1890/91?

11. Which Chelsea player was sent off in the 2008 Champions League final?

12. Which Scottish manager won the Champions League as a player with Borussia Dortmund?

13. Underhill is the home ground of which English football club?

14. True or false – Demba Ba failed to find the net in any of the 13 Premier League games that he started alongside Papiss Cissé in 2011/12?

15. Which Manchester City player provided the most assists in the 2011/12 Premier League season?

16. What is the name of Torquay United's home ground?

17. Which two clubs were relegated from the Football League in 2012?

18. Which club did the Bundesliga and German Cup double in 2011/12?

19. In 2011/12, Manchester United set the record for achieving the most points without winning the Premier League. How many did they manage?
    a) 88
    b) 89
    c) 90

20. Which striker committed the most fouls in the 2011/12 Premier League season?
    a) Kevin Davies
    b) Grant Holt
    c) Wayne Rooney

MEDIUM

Answers to Quiz 44: Pot Luck

1. Churchill Downs
2. Roberto Duran
3. Blue
4. José Mourinho
5. Mick Fitzgerald
6. Brighton and Hove Albion
7. Roland Scholten
8. Skiing
9. Gary Cahill
10. 1958
11. Trevor Berbick
12. Scotland and England
13. Aston Villa
14. Kansas City Chiefs
15. Paul Thorburn
16. Robin Söderling
17. Newmarket
18. Berwick Rangers
19. Sweden
20. Sue Barker

Quiz 46: Pot Luck

1. Which New Zealand rugby union international, who scored the only try in the 2011 World Cup final, has the same name as a former England footballer?

2. Who is the youngest player to play international football for England?

3. Javier Sotomayor was a world and Olympic champion in which athletics event?

4. Which four British racecourses don't contain any of the letters from the word race in their name?

5. Who trained the 2004 Grand National winner Amberleigh House?

6. Which country won the third/fourth place play-off at the 2011 Rugby World Cup?

7. La Bomba was the nickname of which champion skier?

8. Which former World Darts Champion went by the unlikely nickname of The Whippet in his younger days?

9. Fire In Babylon is a 2011 film about which sport?

10. Which England all-rounder got into trouble in 2010 after a foul-mouthed Twitter rant about England selector Geoff Miller?

11. The Giants are an MLB baseball team in which American city?

12. Who was the first rider to win the Tour de France in five consecutive years?

13. Which two football teams play their home games at the Allianz Arena?

14. Which rugby union team reached the World Cup final despite behind thrashed 36-0 by their final opponents in the group stage?

15. England played their first ever World Cup game against an Asian team in 1982. Who were their opponents?

16. Which motorsport legend broke both his ankles after falling down a lift shaft in 2010?

17. In a greyhound race, the dog in which trap wears a black jacket?

18. Who was on the losing team in the Champions League final in 2006 and 2008?

19. Who were the first Irish team to reach the group stages of the Europa League?
    a) Dundalk
    b) Derry City
    c) Shamrock Rovers

20. The 2000 film Remember The Titans is about which sport?
    a) American football
    b) baseball
    c) basketball

Answers to Quiz 45: Football

1. Mario Balotelli
2. Craig Brown
3. Slaven Bilic
4. Shane Long
5. 1989 (when Arsenal pipped Liverpool on goals scored)
6. Bayern Munich
7. Alex Ferguson, Kenny Dalglish and George Burley
8. Wigan Athletic
9. Hearts and Hibernian
10. Aston Villa
11. Didier Drogba
12. Paul Lambert
13. Barnet
14. True
15. David Silva
16. Plainmoor
17. Macclesfield Town and Hereford United
18. Borussia Dortmund
19. 89
20. Grant Holt

MEDIUM

Quiz 47: Formula One

1. Which team won 15 of the 16 Formula One races in the 1988 season?

2. Who was the first Indian to drive in a Formula One race?

3. Which country hosted its first Grand Prix in 2005?

4. Who holds the record for the most wins at the Monaco Grand Prix?

5. What is indicated when a marshall waves a yellow and red striped flag?

6. Which rookie driver finished a record-equalling 18 races during the 2011 season?

7. Which driver died during qualifying at the 1994 San Marino Grand Prix, a day before Ayrton Senna died?

8. Who won the 1957 Drivers' Championship at the age of 46?

9. Which British driver started 158 Grands Prix but never won a race, had a pole position or a fastest lap?

10. Can you name the six British drivers who won the British Grand Prix between 1981 and 2011?

11. Malmedy, Rivage, Fagnes and Stavelot are features of which circuit?

12. The circuit that hosts the Canadian Grand Prix is named after which driver?

13. Who beat Alain Prost by just 0.5 points to win the 1984 Drivers' Championship?

14. What nationality is driver Jérôme d'Ambrosio?

15. Which driver has started the most races since the start of Formula One?

16. Who finished third in the Drivers' Championship in both 2010 and 2011?

17. Jenson Button made his Formula One debut with which team?

18. Who was the first Briton to win the Drivers' Championship?

19. Out of 19 Formula One starts in 2011, how many times did Sebastian Vettel start in pole position?
    a) 14
    b) 15
    c) 16

20. In what year did the first Formula One World Championship take place?
    a) 1949
    b) 1950
    c) 1951

MEDIUM

Answers to Quiz 46: Pot Luck

1. Tony Woodcock
2. Theo Walcott
3. High jump
4. Ludlow, Plumpton, Goodwood and Huntingdon
5. Ginger McCain
6. Australia
7. Alberto Tomba
8. Andy Fordham
9. Cricket
10. Dimitri Mascarenhas
11. San Francisco
12. Miguel Indurain
13. Bayern Munich and 1860 Munich
14. England
15. Kuwait
16. Stirling Moss
17. Trap 4
18. Ashley Cole
19. Shamrock Rovers
20. American football

Quiz 48: Pot Luck

1. In darts, what is the lowest score that cannot be finished in three darts?

2. Craig Joubert, Wayne Barnes and Nigel Owens are international referees in which sport?

3. Who scored for Arsenal in their 2006 Champions League final defeat at the hands of Barcelona?

4. Which Arsenal player was sent off in the same game?

5. The Bull is the nickname of which darts player?

6. What nationality is footballer Ricardo Vaz Tê?

7. Which former England international steered Charlton Athletic to the League One title in 2011/12?

8. What are the names of the three weapons used in Olympic fencing?

9. The Green Monster is a feature of which famous baseball stadium?

10. What nationality is the Olympic champion distance runner Kenenisa Bekele?

11. Which Irishman captained the British and Irish Lions on their 2009 tour to South Africa?

12. Goalkeeper David de Gea joined Manchester United from which club?

13. Phil Taylor won every PDC World Darts Championship bar one between 1995 and 2006. Who beat him in the one final he didn't win?

14. Who scored a double century for England in the 2006/07 Ashes Test at Adelaide but still ended up on the losing side?

15. What are the two competition lifts in Olympic weightlifting?

16. What was the first stadium to host the Rugby World Cup final twice?

17. What nationality is Formula One racing driver Charles Pic?

18. In what town is the Royal St George's Golf Club?

19. How many teams took part in the first season of football's Premier League?
    a) 20
    b) 22
    c) 24

20. Who won the 2012 Scottish Cup final?
    a) Hearts
    b) Hibernian
    c) Kilmarnock

Answers to Quiz 47: Formula One

1. Williams
2. Narain Karthikeyan
3. Turkey
4. Ayrton Senna
5. The track surface is slippery
6. Paul di Resta
7. Roland Ratzenberger
8. Juan Manuel Fangio
9. Martin Brundle
10. John Watson, Nigel Mansell, Damon Hill, Johnny Herbert, David Coulthard and Lewis Hamilton
11. Spa-Francorchamps
12. Gilles Villeneuve
13. Niki Lauda
14. Belgian
15. Rubens Barrichello
16. Mark Webber
17. Williams
18. Mike Hawthorn
19. 15
20. 1950

MEDIUM

Quiz 49: Golf

1. The 2010 Ryder Cup was held at which course?

2. Which New Zealander was the first left-hander to win a major?

3. Who started the final round of the 1999 Open 10 shots behind the leader but still went on to win the championship?

4. Which Briton was runner-up at The Masters and The Open in 2010?

5. Who was the captain of the American team at the 2010 Ryder Cup?

6. Which golfer chartered a plane so he could watch Arsenal's 2006 Champions League final and still make his 7.50am tee time at the Irish Open the following morning?

7. Which British golfer earned a degree in art theory and practice while studying at Northwestern University?

8. Who holds the record for the most runner-up finishes at The Open Championship?

9. Who were the four English golfers in Europe's 2010 Ryder Cup team?

10. Which American won his first major at the 2009 Open Championship?

11. Sometimes dubbed 'the fifth major', the Players Championship takes place at which course?

12. Which British golfer won the 2011 World Matchplay title?

13. Prior to Graeme McDowell's victory in 2010, who was the last European to win the US Open?

14. Which Scandinavian finished in a tie for 3rd at the 2012 Masters?

15. Who was the first non-American to win the US PGA Championship?

16. Who was the youngest player to win The Open Championship in the twentieth century?

17. Who were the first father and son combination from continental Europe to play in the Ryder Cup?

18. Which American, whose Christian name is the same as the surname of an England football manager, won the 2011 US PGA Championship?

19. In 2008, who became the first Irishman to win the US PGA Championship?
    a) Padraig Harrington
    b) Graeme McDowell
    c) Rory McIlroy

20. Who has won The Open Championship the most times out of
    a) Jack Nicklaus
    b) Gary Player
    c) Tom Watson

MEDIUM

Answers to Quiz 48: Pot Luck

1. 159
2. Rugby union
3. Sol Campbell
4. Jens Lehmann
5. Terry Jenkins
6. Portuguese
7. Chris Powell
8. Foil, épée, and sabre
9. Fenway Park
10. Ethiopian
11. Paul O'Connell
12. Atlético Madrid
13. John Part
14. Paul Collingwood
15. Snatch and clean and jerk
16. Eden Park
17. French
18. Sandwich
19. 22
20. Hearts

Quiz 50: Pot Luck

1. What is the first English classic horserace of the the year?

2. Which brothers were part of the 2010 European Ryder Cup team?

3. Jaws is the nickname of which former world number one dart player?

4. What was the first Olympic Games opened by Queen Elizabeth II?

5. Sandy Park is the home ground of which Premiership Rugby Club?

6. Who is the youngest golfer to play in the Ryder Cup?

7. Who is the only player to score points in two Rugby World Cup finals?

8. Which Indian driver appeared in one race for Lotus in the 2011 Formula One season?

9. Who is the youngest male player to complete a career tennis grand slam?

10. Who was the manager of Aston Villa when the midlanders won the European Cup in 1982?

11. Which two teams met in the first all-Spanish Champions League final?

12. Golfer Lee Westwood is a fan of which football club?

13. Prior to Robin van Persie in 2011/12, who was the last player to score 30 goals in a Premier League season?

14. Boom Boom is the nickname of which aesthetically pleasing golfer?

15. Who lost five World Darts Championship finals between 1978 and 1988?

16. FC Hollywood is the nickname of which European football club?

17. Who is the youngest British driver to start a Formula One Grand Prix?

18. Which goalkeeper has kept the most clean sheets in the Premier League?

19. Who has made the most appearances at the Open Championship?
    a) Jack Nicklaus
    b) Gary Player
    c) Tom Watson

20. Which massive underdog beat France at the 2011 Rugby World Cup?
    a) Fiji
    b) Samoa
    c) Tonga

Answers to Quiz 49: Golf

1. Celtic Manor
2. Bob Charles
3. Paul Lawrie
4. Lee Westwood
5. Corey Pavin
6. Ian Poulter
7. Luke Donald
8. Jack Nicklaus
9. Lee Westwood, Ian Poulter, Luke Donald and Ross Fisher
10. Stewart Cink
11. Sawgrass
12. Ian Poulter
13. Tony Jacklin
14. Peter Hanson
15. Gary Player
16. Seve Ballesteros
17. Antonio and Ignacio Garrido
18. Keegan Bradley
19. Padraig Harrington
20. Tom Watson

MEDIUM

Quiz 51: Horse Racing

1. Who, in 2012, became the most successful trainer in the history of the Cheltenham Festival?

2. Which three races make up the American Triple Crown?

3. Who was the flat racing Champion Trainer in 2010 and 2011?

4. In what month is the Prix de l'Arc de Triomphe run?

5. Which English classic is run over the longest distance?

6. What was the last horse to win the Cheltenham Gold Cup and the Grand National in the same year?

7. Why was the 2001 Cheltenham Festival cancelled?

8. The Irish Grand National is run at which course?

9. Who rode War of Attrition to victory in the 2006 Cheltenham Gold Cup?

10. Which jockey's autobiography was called The Wayward Lad?

11. Which two races make up the Spring Double?

12. The Winter Derby is run at which racecourse?

13. Between 2005 and 2012 only three horses won the World Hurdle at Cheltenham. Inglis Drever and Big Buck's were two but who was the third?

14. Who was the last amateur rider to win the Grand National?

15. What horse won the Queen Mother Champion Chase at Cheltenham in 2008 and 2009?

16. What is the minimum age at which a horse can run in the Grand National?

17. What is the most westerly racecourse in mainland Britain?

18. Between 1982 and 2012 only two horses that won the Grand National had names that started with a vowel. Name them.

19. What was the name of the horse that won the first Grand National in 1839?
    a) Jackpot
    b) Lottery
    c) Lucky

20. Which jockey rode the most winners at the 2012 Cheltenham Festival?
    a) Barry Geraghty
    b) Tony McCoy
    c) Ruby Walsh

MEDIUM

Answers to Quiz 50: Pot Luck

1. 1,000 Guineas
2. Francesco and Edoardo Molinari
3. Colin Lloyd
4. Montreal 1976
5. Exeter Chiefs
6. Sergio García
7. Jonny Wilkinson
8. Karun Chandhok
9. Rafael Nadal
10. Tony Barton
11. Real Madrid and Valencia in 2000
12. Nottingham Forest
13. Cristiano Ronaldo
14. Fred Couples
15. John Lowe
16. Bayern Munich
17. Jenson Button
18. David James
19. Gary Player
20. Tonga

Quiz 52: Pot Luck

1. Darth Maple is the nickname of which dart player?

2. Where do the Italian rugby union team usually play their home games?

3. In greyhound racing, what colour jacket is worn by the dog in trap five?

4. At which sporting venue will you see Hogan Bridge, Nelson Bridge and Sarazan Bridge?

5. In a Formula One race, how many points are awarded for a seventh place finish?

6. Which Czech player did Rafael Nadal beat in the 2010 Wimbledon final?

7. Aston Villa owner Randy Lerner is also the owner of which NFL team?

8. Which twins won the Men's Doubles at Wimbledon in 2006 and 2011?

9. Which city hosts a football derby between Flamengo and Fluminese?

10. Roy Hodgson's first game as England manager was a friendly against which team?

11. The Bambino was the nickname of which baseball legend?

12. Who won the 2010 Open Golf Championship by a massive margin of 7 shots?

13. How many teams in the 2011/12 rugby union Aviva Premiership played their home games at football grounds?

14. What was the first country to host the World Cup twice?

15. Who were the four British boxers to fight Muhammad Ali?

16. What is the most northerly racecourse in Britain?

17. Gianluca Vialli managed Chelsea and what other English football club?

18. In what year did Sir Steve Redgrave win his first Olympic gold medal?

19. Jason Lee, star of TV comedy My Name Is Earl, was a professional in which sport?
    a) Rodeo
    b) Skateboarding
    c) Surfing

20. How old was Rory McIlroy when he won his first major?
    a) 21
    b) 22
    c) 23

MEDIUM

Answers to Quiz 51: Horse Racing

1. Nicky Henderson
2. Kentucky Derby, Preakness Stakes, Belmont Stakes
3. Richard Hannon
4. October
5. The St Leger
6. Golden Miller
7. An outbreak of foot and mouth disease
8. Leopardstown
9. Conor O'Dwyer
10. Graham Bradley
11. The Lincoln Handicap and the Grand National
12. Lingfield
13. My Way De Solzen
14. Marcus Armytage
15. Master Minded
16. 6
17. Newton Abbot
18. Amberleigh House and Earth Summit
19. Lottery
20. Ruby Walsh

Quiz 53: Motorsport

1. Who gave the Williams F1 team their first win since 2004 at the 2012 Spanish Grand Prix?

2. Who was the first Russian to drive in Formula One?

3. Since 2001 the British leg of the Speedway Grand Prix has taken place at which venue?

4. Which British driver won the Le Mans 24 Hour Race five times between 1975 and 1987?

5. What do the initials NASCAR stand for?

6. Niki Lauda is one of two Austrians to have won the Formula One Drivers' Championship. Who is the other?

7. Which Spanish rider won the 2011 Superbike World Championship?

8. Which Briton won the 1992 Speedway World Championship?

9. Which British speedway rider was killed after a crash in Poland in May 2012?

10. Which former Formula One driver drove for Earnhardt Ganassi Racing in the NASCAR Sprint Cup Series in 2012?

11. Who is the only South African to win the Formula One Drivers' Championship?

12. Which Elite League Speedway team host meetings at Perry Barr dog track?

13. Which British rider won the Superbike World Championship in 1998 and 1999?

14. Which British driver was killed at the IndyCar 300 in Las Vegas in 2011?

15. Who won the 2011 NASCAR Sprint Cup Championship?

16. Which French driver won the World Touring Car Championship in 2010 and 2011?

17. Timo Glock and Charles Pic drove for which Formula One team in 2012?

18. Which two British circuits hosted World Superbike events in 2012?

19. Lasting over 4 hours, the longest race in Formula One history took place in 2011 in which country?
    a) Canada
    b) Malaysia
    c) Singapore

20. What is the record for the most Formula One wins by a driver in a single Formula One season?
    a) 11
    b) 12
    c) 13

Answers to Quiz 52: Pot Luck

1. John Part
2. Stadio Flaminio
3. Orange
4. Augusta National Golf Club
5. 6 points
6. Tomáš Berdych
7. Cleveland Browns
8. Bob and Mike Bryan
9. Rio de Janeiro
10. Norway
11. Babe Ruth
12. Louis Oosthuizen
13. Four
14. Mexico
15. Henry Cooper, Brian London, Joe Bugner and Richard Dunn
16. Perth
17. Watford
18. 1984
19. Skateboarding
20. 22

Quiz 54: Pot Luck

1. The 2014 Winter Olympics will be held in which country?

2. At which racecourse will you find the Knavesmire?

3. What colour is the outer ring of an archery target?

4. How many players are in an Australian Rules Football team?

5. Who are the two players to have won the World Darts Championship whose surname starts with a vowel?

6. What was the first city to host the Summer Olympics more than once?

7. Who is the youngest person to reach the semi-final in the Ladies' Singles at Wimbledon?

8. Which England rugby player's autobiography was called Me and My Mouth?

9. Stuart Pearce's only game as England manager was a 2-3 defeat at the hands of which country?

10. The lowest attendance in the Premier League in the 2011/12 season was at a game at which ground?

11. The Westfalenstadion is the home ground of which German football club?

12. Who were the first English side to win rugby union's Heineken Cup?

13. At what racecourse is the Cesarewitch Handicap run?

14. Who were the first British club to win the Inter City Fairs Cup?

15. Who are the three South African golfers to have won The Masters?

16. Prior to Linford Christie, who was the last Briton to win gold in the men's Olympic 100m?

17. What nationality are cricket umpires Asad Rauf and Aleem Dar?

18. Which team finished third in their first football World Cup appearance in 1998?

19. Which country has hosted the Commonwealth Games the most times?
    a) Australia
    b) Canada
    c) New Zealand

20. In what year was the Grand National declared void after a false start?
    a) 1992
    b) 1993
    c) 1994

MEDIUM

Answers to Quiz 53: Motorsport

1. Pastor Maldonado
2. Vitaly Petrov
3. Millennium Stadium
4. Derek Bell
5. National Association for Stock Car Auto Racing
6. Jochen Rindt
7. Carlos Checa
8. Gary Havelock
9. Lee Richardson
10. Juan Pablo Montoya
11. Jody Scheckter
12. Birmingham Brummies
13. Carl Fogarty
14. Dan Wheldon
15. Tony Stewart
16. Yvan Muller
17. Marussia
18. Silverstone and Brands Hatch
19. Canada
20. 13

Quiz 55: Olympic Games

1. Which cricket ground was the main venue for a Summer Olympics?

2. Prior to Rebecca Adlington in 2008, who was the last British woman to win an Olympic swimming gold?

3. Which Canadian sprinter won the 1996 men's 100m gold medal?

4. What is the English translation of the Olympic motto, 'Citius, Altius, Fortius'?

5. Which three American cities have hosted the Summer Olympics?

6. Who was the first British woman to win Olympic gold in two different sports?

7. Gail Emms and Nathan Robertson won Olympic medals at which sport?

8. Who retired unbeaten, at the age of just 22, after winning gold in the 1,500m at the 1960 Games?

9. Which country won the Olympic men's football tournament in 2004 and 2008?

10. Over how many rounds is a male Olympic boxing match contested?

11. Which pair were Great Britain's only gold medal winners at the 1996 Olympics?

12. What are the four cities to have hosted the Summer Olympics more than once?

13. Which future world heavyweight champion did Lennox Lewis face in the 1988 Olympic Super Heavyweight final?

14. Over how many rounds is a female Olympic boxing match contested?

15. Who were the four members of Britain's 2004 gold medal winning 4x100m relay team?

16. How many points does a player need to earn to win a game of Olympic table tennis?

17. Which country has won the most medals in the history of the Olympic Games?

18. Ian Percy and Andrew Simpson won Olympic gold in 2008 in which sport?

19. Which country has hosted the Summer Olympics the most times?
    a) France
    b) Great Britain
    c) USA

20. What was the first country to host both the Summer and Winter Olympics?
    a) France
    b) Italy
    c) USA

MEDIUM

Answers to Quiz 54: Pot Luck

1. Russia
2. York
3. White
4. 18
5. Martin Adams and Bob Anderson
6. Paris in 1900 and 1924
7. Jennifer Capriati
8. Austin Healey
9. Holland
10. QPR's Loftus Road
11. Borussia Dortmund
12. Bath
13. Newmarket
14. Leeds United
15. Gary Player, Trevor Immelman and Charl Schwartzel
16. Alan Wells
17. Pakistani
18. Croatia
19. Australia
20. 1993

Quiz 56: Pot Luck

1. Who was the famous owner of the 1994 Grand National winner Miinnehoma?

2. Who was the runner-up in the first World Darts Championship final?

3. Which Finn won Olympic gold in the 5,000m and 10,000m at the 1972 and 1976 Olympics?

4. Fabio Capello was in charge of which club before taking the England manager's job?

5. Which Canadian did Carl Froch beat in 2008 to claim the WBC super middleweight title?

6. Which South African winger scored a record-equalling 8 tries at the 2007 Rugby World Cup?

7. What is the third event of an Olympic decathlon?

8. The Coronation Cup is run at which racecourse?

9. Which three English football clubs have won the UEFA Cup?

10. Which jockey won The Derby on Oath in 1999, Kris Kin in 2003 and North Light in 2004?

11. Which former England cricketer wrote Luck: What it Means and Why it Matters?

12. Who did Tony Pulis succeed as manager of Stoke City in 2006?

13. At which racecourse is the King George VI and Queen Elizabeth Stakes run?

14. Katherine Brunt and Holly Colvin are England internationals in which sport?

15. What is the name of the golf competition that sees a team from GB and Ireland take on a team from continental Europe?

16. Manchester United's biggest ever victory was a 10-0 thrashing of which Belgian club?

17. Who is the host of Radio 5's sporting panel show Fighting Talk?

18. Who were the last Scottish football club to win a European trophy?

19. The England rugby union team's heaviest defeat was a 76-0 drubbing in 1998 at the hands of which opposition?
    a) Australia
    b) New Zealand
    c) South Africa

20. At what age did Björn Borg retire from tennis?
    a) 26
    b) 27
    c) 28

Answers to Quiz 55: Olympic Games

1. Melbourne Cricket Ground in 1956
2. Anita Lonsbrough
3. Donovan Bailey
4. Faster, higher, stronger
5. St Louis, Atlanta and Los Angeles
6. Rebecca Romero
7. Badminton
8. Herb Elliott
9. Argentina
10. Three x three minute rounds
11. Steve Redgrave and Matthew Pinsent
12. Athens, London, Los Angeles and Paris
13. Riddick Bowe
14. Four x 2 minute rounds
15. Jason Gardener, Darren Campbell, Marlon Devonish and Mark Lewis-Francis
16. 11 (and by 2 clear points)
17. USA
18. Sailing
19. USA
20. France

Quiz 57: Books

1. It's Not About The Bike is the award-winning autobiography of which cyclist?

2. Who wrote Beware of the Dog: Rugby's Hard Man Reveals All?

3. A familiar face in front of the cameras, who wrote Jelleyman's Thrown a Wobbly: Saturday Afternoons in Front of the Telly?

4. Booze, Brawls, Sex and Scandal is the title of the autobiography of which wild man of rugby league?

5. Mad Dog: An Englishman is the autobiography of which rugby player?

6. Which legendary cyclist is the subject of Sex, Lies and Handlebar Tape?

7. It Is What It Is is the autobiography of which veteran racing driver?

8. Which footballer revealed all in Tackling My Demons?

9. The Bald Truth – My Life in the World's Hardest Sport is the autobiography of which rugby league player?

10. Which British boxer took The Hard Road to Glory?

11. Who, according to Paul McGuigan and Paolo Hewitt was, The Greatest Footballer You Never Saw?

12. Which footballer was the subject of Glorious: My World, Football and Me?

13. Which father and son combo penned Rocket Men?

14. Which footballer was the subject of The Rebel Who Would Be King?

15. Behind The White Ball was the story of which snooker player's life?

16. Which English cricketer was the subject of a biography called The Power and the Glory?

17. Farewell but not Goodbye was the autobiography of which much travelled football manager?

18. Which Manchester City legend was a Reluctant Hero?

19. Who penned Bellies and Bullseyes: The Outrageous True Story of Darts?

20. Black, White and Gold was the autobiography of which British Olympian?

MEDIUM

Answers to Quiz 56: Pot Luck

1. Freddie Starr
2. John Lowe
3. Lasse Virén
4. Real Madrid
5. Jean Pascal
6. Bryan Habana
7. Shot put
8. Epsom
9. Liverpool, Tottenham and Ipswich Town
10. Kieren Fallon
11. Ed Smith
12. Johan Boskamp
13. Ascot
14. Cricket
15. Seve Trophy
16. Anderlecht
17. Colin Murray
18. Aberdeen
19. Australia
20. 26

Quiz 58: Pot Luck

1. As well as being the home of the All England Lawn Tennis Club, Wimbledon is also home to the All England Club of what other sport?

2. Italy won one match in the 2011 Six Nations Rugby Championship. Which team did they beat?

3. Who is the only athlete to win gold medals in the 5,000m, 10,000m and the marathon in the same Olympic Games?

4. Which English rugby team has won the Premiership the most times?

5. Which goalkeeper scored in a Premier League game against Bolton in January 2012?

6. Who were Britain's two gold medal winners at the 2009 World Athletics Championships?

7. Who was the manager of AC Milan's 1993/94 Champions League winning team?

8. What nationality is US Open tennis champion Samantha Stosur?

9. In which city is the Luzhniki Stadium?

10. Natasha Danvers won a bronze medal at which track event at the 2008 Olympics?

11. Why did the 1997 Grand National take place on a Monday?

12. Who played against the British and Irish Lions with Wellington in 2005 then for the Lions on their 2009 tour to South Africa?

13. In which sport could a player score 'a bag of nails'?

14. Who are the two football managers to have won the Champions League and the World Cup?

15. In what sport can a player be awarded the Bart Starr Award?

16. David Beckham received red cards while playing for England against which two teams?

17. Why did 66 countries boycott the 1980 Olympics in Moscow?

18. Tom Coughlin is a two-time Super Bowl winning coach with which NFL team?

19. In which city was boxer Joe Calzaghe born?
    a) Cardiff
    b) London
    c) Glasgow

20. Excluding the USA, golfers from which country have won the most Majors?
    a) England
    b) Ireland
    c) Scotland

MEDIUM

Answers to Quiz 57: Books

Quiz 59: Rugby Union

1. Who were the only English club to reach the knock-out stages of the 2012 Heineken Cup?

2. What is the name of the trophy which is awarded to winners of Test matches between Australia and New Zealand?

3. The Brumbies are a rugby union team based in which Australian city?

4. What nationality is the referee Alain Rolland?

5. Who holds the record for the most appearances in the Six Nations Championship?

6. In 2002, which team became the first to successfully defend the Heineken Cup?

7. Who was the England coach at the 1999 Rugby World Cup?

8. Who has scored the most Test match tries for the British and Irish Lions?

9. Danny Cipriani had a spell in Australia playing for which team?

10. Which two international teams compete for the Giuseppe Garibaldi Trophy?

11. Which England player had a try disallowed in the 2007 World Cup final?

12. Who holds the record for scoring the most drop goals in international matches?

13. Who are the only Welsh team to reach the final of the Heineken Cup?

14. Which French side did Harlequins beat to claim the 2011 European Challenge Cup?

15. Who was England's youngest ever captain?

16. Which South African was the leading point-scorer at the 2011 Rugby World Cup?

17. Which team finished bottom of the 2011/12 Aviva Premiership?

18. Who are the five players to have scored over 1,000 international points?

19. Who was the first black player to play for Scotland?
    a) David Ansbro
    b) Joe Ansbro
    c) John Ansbro

20. Ronan O'Gara and Brian O'Driscoll are two of the three Irishmen with 100 Test caps. Who is the third?
    a) John Hayes
    b) Peter Stringer
    c) Malcolm O'Kelly

Answers to Quiz 58: Pot Luck

1. Croquet
2. France
3. Emil Zátopek
4. Leicester Tigers
5. Tim Howard
6. Phillips Idowu and Jessica Ennis
7. Fabio Capello
8. Australian
9. Moscow
10. 400m hurdles
11. There was a bomb scare on the Saturday which caused a postponement
12. Riki Flutey
13. Darts
14. Marcello Lippi and Vicente del Bosque
15. American football
16. Argentina and Austria
17. In protest at the Soviet invasion of Afghanistan
18. New York Giants
19. London
20. Scotland

MEDIUM

Quiz 60: Pot Luck

1. What race was won by Kinda Ready in 2009, Bandicot Tipoki in 2010 and Taylors Sky in 2011?

2. The England rugby union team ran up their largest ever victory, 134-0, against which team?

3. In Australian Rules Football, how many points are awarded for a goal?

4. Which country has won tennis's Davis Cup the most times?

5. What is the name of the Ryder Cup-style pool event featuring teams from Europe and the USA?

6. Who was the first black player to play at the World Snooker Championship?

7. Jenny Meadows won a bronze medal at the 2009 World Athletics Championships in which event?

8. Which London-born midfielder played in all five of Turkey's matches at Euro 2008?

9. Which veteran football coach was appointed manager of Russian side Anzhi in 2012?

10. Ridden by Jason Maguire and trained by Donald McCain Jr, which horse won the 2011 Grand National?

11. Rod Macqueen coached which team to victory in the Rugby World Cup?

12. Which defender has scored in the Premier League for Wimbledon, Charlton, Ipswich, Crystal Palace and Portsmouth?

13. Kingston Park is the home ground of which English rugby union team?

14. Who was the last winner of the Ladies' Singles at Wimbledon whose surname starts with a vowel?

15. Who are the three Finns to have won the Formula One Drivers' Championship?

16. Uttoxter racecourse is in which English county?

17. Which country reached the Rugby World Cup quarter-finals in 1987, 1991, 1995, 2003 and 2011 but lost every time?

18. Who was the last winner of the Men's Singles at the Australian Open whose surname starts with a vowel?

19. Briton Alistair Brownlee is a world champion at which sport?

20. Stark's Park is the home ground of which Scottish football club?
    a) Airdrie
    b) Morton
    c) Raith Rovers

21. Which ground hosted the 2006 rugby league Challenge Cup final?
    a) Elland Road
    b) Old Trafford
    c) Twickenham

MEDIUM

Answers to Quiz 59: Rugby Union

1. Saracens
2. Bledisloe Cup
3. Canberra
4. Irish
5. Ronan O'Gara
6. Leicester
7. Sir Clive Woodward
8. Tony O'Reilly
9. Melbourne Rebels
10. Italy and France
11. Mark Cueto
12. Jonny Wilkinson
13. Cardiff in 1996
14. Stade Français
15. Will Carling
16. Morne Steyn
17. Newcastle
18. Dan Carter, Jonny Wilkinson, Ronan O'Gara, Neil Jenkins and Diego Dominguez
19. Joe Ansbro
20. John Hayes

Quiz 61: Snooker

1. After many years at the Wembley Arena, the 2012 Masters was held at what venue?

2. Who won the first World Championship held at the Crucible?

3. Which Australian is the only man to be whitewashed in a World Championship match at the Crucible?

4. The biggest margin of victory in the World Championship final is 18-3. Who was on the losing end against Steve Davis?

5. Who was the first woman to referee a match at the World Championship?

6. Who was the only Englishman to win the World Championship between 1990 and 2000?

7. Which player changed his surname to Brown as part of a sponsorship deal with sauce makers HP?

8. Which Scot won the 2006 World Championship?

9. The first all-Asian Masters final took place in 2011. Which two players were involved?

10. Who accused Ronnie O'Sullivan of disrespecting him after the Rocket played against him left-handed?

11. Who won the world title in 1979 in only his second professional tournament?

12. Taking A Punt On My Life is the title of which snooker player's autobiography?

13. Ding Junhui beat which veteran to claim the 2005 UK Championship?

14. The first World Championship match involving two Asian players took place in 1999. Which two players were involved?

15. Who is the only player to win the world title at junior, amateur and professional level?

16. Who accused China's Cao Yupeng of cheating during a 2012 World Championship match?

17. How long was the longest frame in Crucible history?
    a) 55 minutes
    b) 65 minutes
    c) 75 minutes

18. How many Asian players took part in the 2012 World Championship?
    a) 3
    b) 4
    c) 5

19. Which player is nicknamed The Sheriff of Pottingham?

20. Which midlander was beaten by Stephen Hendry in the 1995 World Championship final?

Answers to Quiz 60: Pot Luck

1. The Greyhound Derby
2. Romania
3. 6
4. USA
5. The Mosconi Cup
6. Rory McLeod
7. 800m
8. Colin Kazim-Richards
9. Guus Hiddink
10. Ballabriggs
11. Australia
12. Herman Hreidarsson
13. Newcastle Falcons
14. Chris Evert
15. Mika Häkkinen, Keke Rosberg and Kimi Räikkönen
16. Staffordshire
17. Ireland
18. Andre Agassi
19. Triathlon
20. Raith Rovers
21. Twickenham

Quiz 62: Pot Luck

1. Which author described sport as 'war minus the shooting'?

2. The Athletics are a baseball team from which American city?

3. Which English pair won the Wimbledon Mixed Doubles Championship in 1987?

4. Which Welshman was the leading point scorer in the 2012 Six Nations Championship?

5. Kirk Edwards plays international cricket for which team?

6. Who was the last Briton to win the 500cc World Motorcycle Riders' Championship?

7. Who succeeded Sir Clive Woodward as coach of the England rugby union team?

8. Steve McLaren won the Dutch championship with which football club?

9. Which former England goalkeeper and manager of Bishop's Stortford is now a coach at Shanghai Shenhua?

10. Philips Stadion is the home ground of which European football club?

11. The Executioner was the nickname of which boxer?

12. Which Welsh rugby player appeared on reality TV show Celebrity Big Brother in 2012?

13. The Willows was the long-time home of which rugby league club?

14. Who was the last player to win the US Masters golf whose surname begins with a vowel?

15. Which country won the 2008 Rugby League World Cup?

16. Andreas Thorkildsen won Olympic gold in 2004 and 2008 in which athletics event?

17. Who is the oldest player to score a goal in the Champions League?

18. Which crew has won the University Boat Race the most times?

19. The uncle of which Grand Slam tennis winner played at the 1996 European Football Championship?
    a) Novak Djokovic
    b) Roger Federer
    c) Rafael Nadal

20. American football matches are played over how many minutes?
    a) 60
    b) 80
    c) 90

MEDIUM

Answers to Quiz 61: Snooker

1. Alexandra Palace
2. John Spencer
3. Eddie Charlton
4. John Parrott
5. Michaela Tabb
6. John Parrott
7. Jimmy White
8. Graeme Dott
9. Ding Junhui and Marco Fu
10. Alain Robidoux
11. Terry Griffiths
12. Willie Thorne
13. Steve Davis
14. Marco Fu and James Wattana
15. Ken Doherty
16. Mark Allen
17. 75 minutes
18. 5
19. Anthony Hamilton
20. Nigel Bond

Quiz 63: Tennis

1. Who ranted at an umpire at the 2011 US Open, saying, 'You're a hater and you're unattractive inside'?

2. Which major winner went out in the first round of a grand slam event for the first time at the 2012 French Open?

3. Who defeated Andy Murray in the 2011 Australian Open final?

4. Who was the last woman to win the Wimbledon Singles, Doubles and Mixed Doubles Championships in the same year?

5. Tim Henman lost four Wimbledon semi-finals to which three players?

6. Which British player won the Wimbledon Junior Girls' Championship in 2007 at the age of 14?

7. Who did Spain beat to win the 2011 Davis Cup?

8. Which tennis player's controversial 2009 autobiography was called Open?

9. In what country was Elena Baltacha born?

10. Which Cypriot smashed four racquets after losing a game is his 2012 Australian Open match against Stanislas Wawrinka?

11. Who was the first black Wimbledon champion?

12. What is the ITF World Mixed Team Championships also known as?

13. Which tennis player has her own nail polish range and clothing line and a charity devoted to helping the victims of violent crime?

14. How many matches must a player win to become Wimbledon Men's Singles champions?

15. Who won the Wimbledon mixed doubles title in 2007 with Jelena Janković?

16. Which Australian did Roger Federer beat to win his first Wimbledon Singles title?

17. In what country was John McEnroe born?

18. Who is the tallest player ever to play at Wimbledon?

19. Who has won the most Ladies' Singles Grand Slam titles?
    a) Steffi Graf
    b) Billie Jean King
    c) Martina Navratilova

20. Players from which country have won the Men's Singles at Wimbledon the most times?
    a) Australia
    b) Great Britain
    c) USA

MEDIUM

Answers to Quiz 62: Pot Luck

1. George Orwell
2. Oakland
3. Jeremy Bates and Jo Durie
4. Leigh Halfpenny
5. West Indies
6. Barry Sheene
7. Andy Robinson
8. FC Twente
9. Ian Walker
10. PSV Eindhoven
11. Bernard Hopkins
12. Gareth Thomas
13. Salford
14. Trevor Immelman in 2008
15. New Zealand
16. Javelin
17. Ryan Giggs
18. Cambridge
19. Rafael Nadal
20. 60

Quiz 64: Pot Luck

1. How many players are there in a Gaelic football team?

2. In horse racing, at what course is the Dante Stakes run?

3. In what country do rugby union teams compete for the Currie Cup?

4. What is fence six at the Grand National better known as?

5. Which England rugby union one-cap wonder scored a record-breaking 75 tries for Sale between 1998 and 2008?

6. What nationality is the jockey Mickael Barzalona?

7. Which two British athletes won the men's and women's long jump at the 1964 Olympics?

8. The Redcar Bears and Ipswich Witches are teams in which sport?

9. Heywood Road was the original home ground of which rugby union club?

10. Which Scot lost in the final of the 2004 World Snooker Championship?

11. Greg Louganis was an Olympic champion in which sport?

12. What colour are the two rings on the bottom row of the Olympic flag?

13. Who were the three teams from outside the County Championship that took part in the 2012 CB 40 cricket competition?

14. Which manager steered Liverpool to victory in the 1984 European Cup final?

15. What is the largest football stadium in Europe?

16. Which country won the 2010 Women's Rugby World Cup?

17. How many matches did Chelsea lose en route to winning the 2011/12 Champions League?

18. Which team beat Rangers in the final of the 2007/08 UEFA Cup?

19. What is the lowest score recorded at The Open Golf Championship?
    a) 62
    b) 63
    c) 64

20. Why was the 2012 University Boat Race disrupted?
    a) a boat sank
    b) a boat was hit by a launch
    c) someone swam between the boats

MEDIUM

Answers to Quiz 63: Tennis

1. Serena Williams
2. Serena Williams
3. Novak Djokovic
4. Billie Jean King in 1973
5. Pete Sampras (twice), Goran Ivanišević and Lleyton Hewitt
6. Laura Robson
7. Argentina
8. Andre Agassi
9. Ukraine
10. Marcos Baghdatis
11. Althea Gibson
12. The Hopman Cup
13. Serena Williams
14. 7
15. Jamie Murray
16. Mark Philippoussis
17. Germany
18. Ivo Karlović
19. Steffi Graf
20. USA

Quiz 65: Trophies

In what sport are the following trophies awarded?

1. Harry Sunderland Trophy

2. Sam Maguire Cup

3. Swaythling Cup

4. Heisman Trophy

5. The Millennium Trophy

6. Grey Cup

7. The Venus Rosewater Dish

8. Caulfield Cup

9. Iroquois Cup

10. Henri Delaunay Cup

11. Frank Worrell Trophy

12. Eisenhower Trophy

13. Sheffield Shield

14. Wightman Cup

15. Commissioner's Trophy

16. Thomas Cup

17. Copa Libertadores

18. Ove Fundin Trophy

19. The Daphne Akhurst Memorial Cup

20. The Wanamaker Trophy

Answers to Quiz 64: Pot Luck

1. 15
2. York
3. South Africa
4. Becher's Brook
5. Steve Hanley
6. French
7. Lynn Davies and Mary Rand
8. Speedway
9. Sale Sharks
10. Graeme Dott
11. Diving
12. Yellow and green
13. Scotland, the Netherlands and Unicorns
14. Joe Fagan
15. Barcelona's Camp Nou
16. New Zealand
17. Two
18. Zenit St Petersburg
19. 63
20. Someone swam between the boats

Quiz 66: Pot Luck

1. What nationality is Formula One racing driver Pastor Maldonado?

2. Provided You Don't Kiss Me is an award-winning biography of which football figure?

3. At what track is the Greyhound Derby run?

4. Which Englishman was the leading scorer in the Scottish Premier League in 2011/12?

5. The 2012 London Paralympics featured how many sports?

6. Which team won baseball's World Series in 2011?

7. What do the AC in AC Milan stand for?

8. In 2008, who became the first British gymnast since 1908 to win an Olympic medal?

9. Which American city is home to professional sports teams called Blackhawks and Cubs?

10. What are the names of the reserve boats in the University Boat Race?

11. Which golfer died in a plane crash shortly after winning the 1999 US Open?

12. Bill Belichick is the head coach of which American football team?

13. How many games did the England football team lose under Fabio Capello in 2011?

14. Jenny Pitman is one of two women to train a Grand National winning horse. Who is the other?

15. What is the only South American country that hosts Test match cricket?

16. Which city will host the 2015 World Athletics Championships?

17. Who captained the New Zealand side that won the 2011 Rugby World Cup?

18. Who was the skip of the British curling team that won gold at the 2002 Winter Olympics?

19. Which club wasn't an original member of the Football League?
    a) Derby County
    b) Leicester City
    c) Notts County

20. Which of the following was not an Olympic sport?
    a) billiards
    b) cricket
    c) croquet

MEDIUM

Answers to Quiz 65: Trophies

1. Rugby league
2. Gaelic football
3. Table tennis
4. American football
5. Rugby union
6. Canadian football
7. Tennis
8. Horse racing
9. Lacrosse
10. Football
11. Cricket
12. Golf
13. Cricket
14. Tennis
15. Baseball
16. Badminton
17. Football
18. Speedway
19. Tennis
20. Golf

Quiz 67: Firsts and Lasts

1. In what year did the first Cricket World Cup take place?

2. What happened in the University Boat Race for the first time in 1912?

3. Which team won the first World Cup final settled by a penalty shoot-out?

4. In 1982, Geraldine Rees became the first woman to do what?

5. In what year did England make their FIFA World Cup debut?

6. Who was the first bowler to take 400 Test match wickets?

7. The last ever European Cup Winners' Cup final was held at which English ground?

8. Who was the first Swedish player to win the Premier League?

9. Who were the first English league club to play in Europe?

10. Who was the last player to win the junior and senior Men's Singles titles at Wimbledon?

11. Which Leeds United striker was the last player to make his England international debut at the World Cup finals?

12. Who in 2000 was the last French player to win a singles title at the French Open tennis?

13. Who were the first English team to beat Real Madrid at the Bernabeu Stadium?

14. Which country won the first UEFA European Championship?

15. Sue Brown was the first woman to participate in which sporting event?

16. In what year did football's European Championship finals last feature just 8 teams?

17. What was the venue for the first Cricket World Cup final not hosted at Lord's?

18. Which England bowler blocked out the last over to secure draws in two Test matches in South Africa in 2009/10?

19. The first Super Bowl took place in what year?
    a) 1965
    b) 1967
    c) 1969

20. In what year did Northern Ireland last appear in the World Cup finals?
    a) 1982
    b) 1986
    c) 1990

MEDIUM

Answers to Quiz 66: Pot Luck

1. Venezuelan
2. Brian Clough
3. Wimbledon
4. Gary Hooper
5. 20
6. St Louis Cardinals
7. Associazione Calcio
8. Louis Smith
9. Chicago
10. Isis and Goldie
11. Payne Stewart
12. New England Patriots
13. None
14. Venetia Williams
15. Guyana
16. Beijing
17. Richie McCaw
18. Rhona Martin
19. Leicester City
20. Billiards

DIFFICULT QUIZZES

Quiz 68: Pot Luck

1. The first Commonwealth Games were held in which country?

2. Scala is the middle name of which England rugby union hooker?

3. What is the only country to have won at least one gold medal at every Summer Olympics?

4. Which South African cricket ground is overlooked by Table Mountain?

5. What name connects a former Liverpool midfielder and the Korean-American winner of Olympic diving medals in 1948 and 1952?

6. Who captained Manchester United in the 1999 Champions League final?

7. Which team finished fourth in the 2007 Rugby World Cup?

8. Monmore Green greyhound track is in which English city?

9. What colour is between the red and black rings on an archery target?

10. Which female athlete won the 1991 BBC Sports Personality of the Year award?

11. What name is shared by a British Olympic high jump bronze medallist and an Australian spin bowler?

12. Which member of Blackburn Rovers' 1995 Premier League winning team is now a qualified solicitor?

13. Who was the first cricketer of Indian origin to play 100 Tests for the West Indies?

14. Paul Lambert's first managerial job in England was with which club?

15. In what year did Great Britain last win the Rugby League World Cup?

16. Who are the two Olympic gold medallists to appear on Strictly Come Dancing?

17. The first Rugby League World Cup was held in which country?

18. Who holds the record for winning the most Olympic gold medals?

19. How many times did Liverpool hit the woodwork in Premier League matches in 2011/12?
    a) 31
    b) 32
    c) 33

20. How many goals did Lionel Messi score in the Spanish League in the 2011/12 season?
    a) 48
    b) 50
    c) 52

Answers to Quiz 100: Pot Luck

1. Equatorial Guinea
2. Biarritz and Toulon
3. Shane Watson
4. Montpellier
5. Aidan O'Brien
6. Authorized
7. John Spencer
8. Angola, Ghana, Togo and Ivory Coast
9. Football
10. Wheelchair rugby
11. 7 - 6 outfield players and a goalkeeper
12. It was a five-way tie after each team won two and lost two matches
13. Men's decathlon
14. Rob Kearney
15. Argentina
16. South Africa and Ivory Coast
17. Bowls
18. Michael Kasprowicz
19. 38
20. Basketball

DIFFICULT

Quiz 69: Athletics

1. Which British athlete won her first international title at the age of 37 when she won gold in the 3,000m at the 2011 European Indoor Championships?

2. Which triple jumper, who had previously won medals for both her native Cuba and Sudan, won gold for Britain at the 2012 World Indoor Championships?

3. Mo Farah set a British record in the 10,000m in 2011. Whose record did he beat?

4. Which British European Championship winning 800m runner went on to become a Strathclyde policeman after retiring from the sport?

5. What is the only British city to have hosted the World Indoor Athletics Championships?

6. Which Cuban became the first man to win the 400m and 800m at the same Olympics at the 1976 Games?

7. Three-time world 800m champion Wilson Kipketer represented which European country?

8. Two men have won nine Olympic gold medals in athletics events. Carl Lewis is one. Which Finn is the other?

9. The British women's 200m record was set at the 1984 Olympics by which athlete?

10. Which British athlete won a bronze medal in the 800m at the 2012 World Indoor Championships?

11. Keith Connor won a bronze medal at the 1984 Olympic Games in which event?

12. Which Briton was named IAAF World Athlete of the Year in 1990?

13. Which British athlete won a silver medal in the 1500m at the 1988 Seoul Olympics?

14. Kenya's David Rudisha won gold at the 2011 World Championships in which event?

15. Who is the only Namibian to win an Olympic medal?

16. Which two British field event athletes won silver medals at the 2008 Olympics?

17. Obadele Thompson won which country's only Olympic medal at the 2000 Games?
    a) Bahamas
    b) Barbados
    c) Bermuda

18. Which Briton won a silver medal in the 200m at the 2000 Olympics?
    a) Darren Campbell
    b) Marlon Devonish
    c) John Regis

19. The 2012 British Olympic trials were held in which city?

20. Tom Parsons represented Great Britain at the 2008 Olympics in which event?

Answers to Quiz 68: Pot Luck

1. Canada
2. George Chuter
3. Great Britain
4. Newlands
5. Sammy Lee
6. Peter Schmeichel
7. France
8. Wolverhampton
9. Blue
10. Liz McColgan
11. Steve Smith
12. Stuart Ripley
13. Shivnarine Chanderpaul
14. Wycombe Wanderers
15. 1972
16. Denise Lewis and Audley Harrison
17. France
18. Swimmer Michael Phelps
19. 33
20. 50

DIFFICULT

Quiz 70: Pot Luck

1. Denisse Astrid van Lamoen, Kim Woojin, Albina Loginova and Christopher Perkins are world champions in which sport?

2. The infamous Battle of Boet Erasmus at the 1995 Rugby World Cup featured players from South Africa and what other country?

3. Who was the first white athlete to break the 10 second barrier in the 100 metres?

4. In 2012, Leicester City agreed a record £1m fee for which non-league player?

5. Before representing Great Britain, long jumper Shara Proctor performed in international competition for which Caribbean country?

6. Which rugby league team reached their first, and so far only, Challenge Cup final in 1999?

7. Which team scored the fewest goals in the 2011/12 Premier League season?

8. Who has won the most US Open Women's Singles titles in the open era (post 1968)?

9. Which European golfer holds the record for the lowest four round score in the US Open?

10. What name is shared by a New Zealand tennis player who reached the Wimbledon final in 1983 and a former England cricket all-rounder?

11. Which Birmingham boxer lost on a controversial split decision to WBA Middleweight champion Felix Sturm in 2011?

12. Sam Allardyce started his managerial career with which Irish club?

13. Blanka Vlašić is a world champion in which athletics event?

14. Who is the leading point scorer in the history of rugby union's Aviva Premiership?

15. What nationality is 5,000m World and Olympic champion Meseret Defar?

16. Which Belgian golfer won the 2012 Volvo World Matchplay Championship?

17. Stade de la Mosson is the home ground of which French football club?

18. Who was the first hooker to captain his team to victory in the Rugby World Cup?

19. The International Olympic Committee is based in which Swiss city?
    a) Berne
    b) Geneva
    c) Lausanne

20. Which country has not appeared in the Rugby League World Cup?
    a) Georgia
    b) Lebanon
    c) Russia

Answers to Quiz 69: Athletics

1. Helen Clitheroe
2. Yamilé Aldama
3. Jon Brown
4. Tom McKean
5. Birmingham
6. Alberto Juantorena
7. Denmark
8. Paavo Nurmi
9. Kathy Cook
10. Andrew Osagie
11. Triple jump
12. Steve Backley
13. Peter Elliott
14. 800m
15. Frankie Fredericks
16. Phillips Idowu and Germaine Mason
17. Barbados
18. Darren Campbell
19. Birmingham
20. High jump

DIFFICULT

Quiz 71: Boxing

1. Prior to James Degale in 2008, who was the last British boxer to win an Olympic middleweight gold medal?

2. Which Dane handed Carl Froch his first professional defeat?

3. Which Irish fighter suffered a 10th round TKO while challenging Lucian Bute for the IBF Super Middleweight title in 2011?

4. Which heavyweight champion was nicknamed the Galveston Giant?

5. Floyd Mayweather Jr has won world titles at which five weight divisions?

6. Which heavyweight is believed to have been the inspiration for the Rocky films?

7. Who in 2012 won Britain's first ever women's boxing world title?

8. Which British world champion was nicknamed The Fighting Carpenter?

9. The Count of Monte Fisto was the nickname of which fictional fighter?

10. Which former world middleweight champion, whose nickname was 'Second To', was jailed on drugs offences in 2004?

11. Which British boxer, who died in 2012, won gold in the flyweight division at the 1956 Olympics?

12. Which American did David Haye beat in his first world heavyweight championship title defence?

13. Which British fighter turned commentator was beaten by Roy Jones Jr in the semi-final of the 1988 Olympic boxing competition?

14. Which brothers, who both went on to win world heavyweight titles, won gold medals at the 1976 Olympic Games?

15. What is Mike Tyson's middle name?

16. Which Liverpudlian super heavyweight won bronze at the 2008 Olympic Games?

17. Which Colombian fighter handed Amir Khan his first professional defeat?

18. Which Mexican light welterweight is nicknamed The Hispanic Causing Panic?

19. Which boxer did not win a gold medal in the heavyweight division at the Olympic Games?
    a) Muhammad Ali
    b) George Foreman
    c) Joe Frazier

20. Medals were awarded in how many weight divisions at the 2012 Olympics?
    a) 8
    b) 10
    c) 12

Answers to Quiz 70: Pot Luck

1. Archery
2. Canada
3. Christophe Lemaître
4. Jamie Vardy
5. Anguilla
6. London Broncos
7. Stoke City
8. Chris Evert
9. Rory McIlroy with a 268 in 2011
10. Chris Lewis
11. Matthew Macklin
12. Limerick
13. High jump
14. Charlie Hodgson
15. Ethiopian
16. Nicolas Colsaerts
17. Montpellier
18. South Africa's John Smit
19. Lausanne
20. Georgia

DIFFICULT

Quiz 72: Pot Luck

1. Who was named man of the match in the 2011 Rugby World Cup final?

2. What was the first Asian city to host the Commonwealth Games?

3. What colour is the jersey worn by the leading sprinter in cycling's Giro d'Italia?

4. Before taking over at Chelsea, André Villas-Boas was the manager of which club?

5. New Zealand ran up a Rugby World Cup record score of 145 points against which opposition?

6. Which two-time World Superbikes Champion announced his retirement from motorsport in 2011 due to a wrist injury?

7. Which two teams failed to find the net in the most games (15) in the 2011/12 Premier League season?

8. What rugby union position is sometimes known in New Zealand as first five-eighth?

9. What is the only NFL team that plays its home games in the state of New York?

10. How many players are in a basketball team?

11. Who was the only player not named Federer, Nadal or Djokovic to win a Grand Slam tennis event between 2006 and 2011?

12. The Conn Smythe Trophy and Jack Adams Award are prizes given in which sport?

13. Anier García, Liu Xiang and Dayron Robles are Olympic gold medallists in which track event?

14. Which country won the Women's Cricket World Cup in 2009?

15. In what year did the Ryder Cup known as 'The War on the Shore' take place?

16. Which England batsman has been involved in the most Test match wins at Lord's?

17. Which South African snooker player served three years in prison for cannabis smuggling?

18. Which Irishman was the leading try scorer in the 2012 Six Nations Rugby Championship?

19. How many different sports featured in the 2012 London Olympics?
    a) 26
    b) 27
    c) 28

20. Which team won rugby union's County Championship in 2009, 2010 and 2011?

Answers to Quiz 71: Boxing

1. Chris Finnegan
2. Mikkel Kessler
3. Brian Magee
4. Jack Johnson
5. Super Featherweight, Lightweight, Light Welterweight, Welterweight, Light Middleweight
6. Chuck Wepner
7. Savannah Marshall
8. Ken Buchanan
9. Apollo Creed from the Rocky films
10. Michael Nunn
11. Terry Spinks
12. John Ruiz
13. Richie Woodhall
14. Leon and Michael Spinks
15. Gerard
16. David Price
17. Breidis Prescott
18. Juan Lazcano
19. Muhammad Ali (he won gold at light heavyweight)
20. 10

DIFFICULT

Quiz 73: Cricket

1. Which country hosted Pakistan's 2012 Test series against England?

2. How many players made their England Test debut in 2011?

3. Who were the three Pakistani cricketers jailed for their involvement in the 2010 spot fixing scandal?

4. Who are the four England bowlers to have taken 7 wickets in a Test match innings against the West Indies at Lord's?

5. Beausejour Stadium is a Test match venue in which Caribbean country?

6. Which South African-born seamer replaced the injured Ajmal Shahzad at the 2011 Cricket World Cup?

7. Who is the youngest player to win a Test cap for New Zealand?

8. Which West Indian was coach of the Irish team that beat England in the 2011 Cricket World Cup?

9. Who are the five Englishmen to appear on both the batting and bowling honours board at Lord's?

10. Who was the first batsman to face 1000 consecutive deliveries without getting out in Test cricket?

11. Which West Indian captain turned county coach was involved in nine Test run outs but was never dismissed himself?

12. Name the four cricketers to have won the BBC Sports Personality of the Year award.

13. Excluding Sachin Tendulkar, who is the youngest batsman to score 5,000 Test runs?

14. England captain Andrew Strauss played a warm-up match for which county against the Indian touring side in 2011?

15. Who was the first player to score One Day International centuries for two countries?

16. Who became the first Lancashire player to take two wickets in his first over for the club in a 2012 Championship match against Sussex?

17. Which member of England's 1981 Ashes winning team now works on the newspaper counter of the Truro branch of Sainsbury's?

18. Which England seamer took two wickets in his first Test over against Zimbabwe in 2003?

19. Who was the first Australian since 1877 to be picked for the national team despite not having player first-class cricket?
    a) Pat Cummins
    b) Clint McKay
    c) David Warner

20. Who was the first England bowler to dismiss Sachin Tendulkar, Rahul Dravid and Sourav Ganguly in the same innings?
    a) James Anderson
    b) Stuart Broad
    c) Graeme Swann

Answers to Quiz 72: Pot Luck

1. Thierry Dusautoir
2. Kuala Lumpur
3. Red
4. Porto
5. Japan
6. James Toseland
7. Aston Villa and Swansea
8. Fly-half
9. Buffalo Bills (the NY Giants and NY Jets play in New Jersey)
10. 5
11. Juan Martín del Potro
12. Ice hockey
13. 110m hurdles
14. England
15. 1991
16. Andrew Strauss
17. Silvino Francisco
18. Tommy Bowe
19. 26
20. Lancashire

DIFFICULT

151

Quiz 74: Pot Luck

1. Which country made its Rugby World Cup debut at the 2011 tournament?

2. Who was the only goalkeeper to save a penalty from Matthew Le Tissier?

3. Which lawn bowler took part in eight Commonwealth Games between 1974 and 2010?

4. The Orioles are a baseball team in which American city?

5. What is the name of the golf competition that features amateur women's teams from the USA and Great Britain and Ireland?

6. England rugby internationals Delon and Steffon Armitage were born in which country?

7. How did Australian Michael O'Brien make history at a rugby international between England and France at Twickenham in 1974?

8. What are the three NFL teams in the state of Florida?

9. Blackledge is the middle name of which former England rugby union captain?

10. Which city hosted the 2012 World Indoor Athletics Championships?

11. Teófilo Stevenson, the first man to win three consecutive Olympic heavyweight gold medals, represented which country?

12. Which former England cricket captain was involved in 8 Test match run outs that saw his partner dismissed seven times?

13. Which Italian football club play their home games at Stadio San Paolo?

14. Which team ran out 106-12 victors over Bedford in an English Premiership rugby match in 1999?

15. Who was the first athlete to break the 10 second barrier in the 100 metres?

16. In what English county do the Badminton Horse Trials take place?

17. In 1992, Gareth Marriott became the first Briton to win an Olympic medal in which sport?

18. Durham Wildcats, Glasgow Rocks and Guildford Heat are teams in which sport?

19. In which city will you find an Australian rules football team called the Crows?
    a) Adelaide
    b) Brisbane
    c) Canberra

20. Former Ireland coach Eddie O'Sullivan was in charge of which team at the 2011 Rugby World Cup?
    a) Georgia
    b) Tonga
    c) USA

Answers to Quiz 73: Cricket

1. United Arab Emirates
2. None
3. Mohammad Amir, Mohammad Asif and Salman Butt
4. Trevor Bailey, Ian Botham, Dominic Cork and Stuart Broad
5. St Lucia
6. Jade Dernbach
7. Daniel Vettori
8. Phil Simmons
9. Gubby Allen, Ian Botham, Stuart Broad, Andrew Flintoff and Ray Illingworth
10. Shivnarine Chanderpaul
11. Jimmy Adams
12. Jim Laker, David Steele, Ian Botham and Andrew Flintoff
13. Alastair Cook
14. Somerset
15. Eoin Morgan (for Ireland and England)
16. Ajmal Shahzad
17. Chris Old
18. Richard Johnson
19. David Warner
20. James Anderson

DIFFICULT

Quiz 75: Cycling

1. Which Frenchman has won the Tour de France King of the Mountains competition the most times?

2. Which Uzbeki sprint cyclist was nicknamed The Tashkent Terror?

3. Who was the first non-European to win the Tour de France?

4. Which two British riders finished on the podium in the 2011 Tour of Spain?

5. Who is the only American to win the Giro d'Italia?

6. Which Briton won the bronze medal in the 1996 Men's Olympic Road Race?

7. Which of cycling's Classic races is known as l'Enfer du Nord (Hell of the North)?

8. Who was the last rider to win the Tour de France and Giro d'Italia in the same year?

9. Who was the first British rider to win a stage in the Tour de France?

10. What is the only one-day Classic held in Holland?

11. The first Classic of the year is a race between Milan and which city?

12. Which former Tour de France winner joined Spanish second division football club Coruxo after retiring from cycling?

13. Monsieur Chrono was the nickname of which French cycling legend?

14. After Paris, which city has hosted the Tour de France the most times?

15. Which British rider finished second behind Chris Hoy in the 2008 Olympic keirin race?

16. Up to 2011, who were the four British riders to have worn the Tour de France yellow jersey?

17. What race, sometimes known as La Doyenne, is the oldest of cycling's Classic races?

18. Which French rider won the Tour de France in 1975 and 1977?

19. The 2012 Giro d'Italia started in which country?
    a) Denmark
    b) Norway
    c) Sweden

20. Of the ten track cycling gold medals available at the 2008 Olympics, how many were won by British riders?
    a) 5
    b) 6
    c) 7

Answers to Quiz 74: Pot Luck

1. Russia
2. Mark Crossley
3. Willie Wood
4. Baltimore
5. Curtis Cup
6. Trinidad and Tobago
7. He was the first person to streak at a UK sporting event
8. Miami Dolphins, Jacksonville Jaguars and Tampa Bay Buccaneers
9. Bill Beaumont
10. Istanbul
11. Cuba
12. Nasser Hussain
13. Napoli
14. Richmond
15. Jim Hines
16. Gloucestershire
17. Canoeing
18. Basketball
19. Adelaide
20. USA

DIFFICULT

Quiz 76: Pot Luck

1. Who won the BBC Sports Personality of the Year Coach Award in 2011?

2. Who are the two players other than Phil Taylor to have won the Premier League Darts title?

3. Who was the first female tennis player to win the Grand Slam and an Olympic gold medal in the same year?

4. In 1907, Arnaud Massy became the first foreign winner of which famous sporting event?

5. How many players are there in a handball team?

6. Which former policeman scored twice for Great Britain in the 1988 Olympic hockey final?

7. Who is the trainer of the record-breaking horse Frankel?

8. In what city is the rugby stadium Ellis Park?

9. Who beat Carl Froch in the final of the Super Six World Boxing Classic?

10. Who was the first England cricketer to take a hat-trick in a One Day International?

11. In 2000, Stacy Dragila became the first Olympic gold medal winner in which athletics event?

12. Who was the first foreigner to manage a top-flight English football club?

13. Who was the highest placed British finisher in the 2011 Tour de France?

14. Who was the only Briton to reach the final of the men's 200m at the Beijing Olympics?

15. In what year did the West Indies last win a Test match at Lord's?

16. Who was the first European to win The Masters golf tournament?

17. What is the only Belgian city to host the Olympic Games?

18. Who is the only Australian cricketer to appear on the batting and bowling honours board at Lord's?

19. Which country won the Speedway World Cup in 2011?
    a) Australia
    b) Denmark
    c) Poland

20. Scotland failed to reach the quarter-final of the 2011 Rugby World Cup, ending a streak of how many successive last eight appearances?
    a) 4
    b) 5
    c) 6

Answers to Quiz 75: Cycling

1. Richard Virenque
2. Djamolidine Abdoujaparov
3. Greg Lemond
4. Chris Froome and Bradley Wiggins
5. Andy Hampsten
6. Max Sciandri
7. Paris-Roubaix
8. Marco Pantani
9. Brian Robinson
10. Amstel Gold
11. San Remo
12. Óscar Pereiro
13. Jacques Anquetil
14. Bordeaux
15. Ross Edgar
16. Tom Simpson, Chris Boardman, Sean Yates, David Millar
17. Liège-Bastogne-Liège
18. Bernard Thévenet
19. Denmark
20. 6

DIFFICULT

Quiz 77: Darts

1. Who are the five Welshman to have reached a World Championship final?

2. Which Thai-born American reached the semi-final of the 1978 World Championship?

3. Raymond van Barneveld is from which Dutch city?

4. Which outsider did John Part beat in the 2008 PDC World Championship final?

5. Who is the only player to play international darts for three countries?

6. Who was the first left-handed player to win the World Championship?

7. James Wade beat which American to take the 2008 UK Open title?

8. Who came back from 6-0 down to tie the score at 6-6 in the 2007 BDO World Championship final but ended up losing 7-6 to Martin Adams?

9. Which former World Champion has a street named in his honour?

10. Which televised PDC tournament requires players to double in and double out?

11. Which Yorkshireman did Martin Adams beat in the 2011 BDO World Championship final?

12. Which World Champion is also a qualified driving instructor?

13. Which player lost in both of his World Championship final appearances in 1984 and 1986?

14. Who won the 2012 Women's World Championship?

15. In 1985, who became the first player to average over 100 in a World Championship match?

16. Which outsider won the 2010 Grand Slam of Darts?

17. Who, in 2006, became the youngest winner of the Winmau World Masters?

18. Bobby George reached the 1994 BDO final after winning an epic semi-final against which Swedish player?

19. Who was the first player to hit a televised nine-dart finish?
    a) Eric Bristow
    b) John Lowe
    c) Jocky Wilson

20. The first ever World Darts Championship took place in which city?
    a) Leicester
    b) Nottingham
    c) Stoke-on-Trent

Answers to Quiz 76: Pot Luck

1. Andy Flower
2. James Wade and Gary Anderson
3. Steffi Graf
4. The Open Golf Championship
5. 7
6. Imran Sherwani
7. Henry Cecil
8. Johannesburg
9. Andre Ward
10. James Anderson
11. Women's pole vault
12. Dr Jozef Vengloš
13. Geraint Thomas
14. Christian Malcolm
15. 1988
16. Seve Ballesteros
17. Antwerp
18. Keith Miller
19. Poland
20. 6

DIFFICULT

Quiz 78: Pot Luck

1. The Ranfurly Shield is a domestic rugby union competition in which country?

2. The Queen's Park Oval is a cricket ground in which Caribbean capital?

3. Who in 2012 became the 10th batsman to score 10,000 Test match runs?

4. Which pair shared 19 wickets (the other was a run out) in England's 2006 Test victory over Pakistan at Old Trafford in 2006?

5. How many players are there in a baseball team?

6. Which British athlete reached the final of the men's 400m at the 2008 Olympic Games?

7. The Palio is a horse race that takes place in which Italian city?

8. Which team were promoted to the Football League in the 2012 Conference play-off final?

9. Which team did they beat in the final?

10. Which sporting event provided the title of a 2003 album by German techno giants Kraftwerk?

11. Louis Smith won Britain's first men's Olympic gymnastics medal for 80 years in 2008 on which piece of apparatus?

12. Wigan's Aylesbury-born defender Emmerson Boyce has played international football for which country?

13. Which Irishman did Phil Taylor beat in the final of the 2011 World Grand Prix darts tournament?

14. Which former England striker was born in French Guiana?

15. Who managed Bristol Rovers between 1996 and 2001?

16. Who was named Man of the Series in the in cricket's World T20 tournament in 2010?

17. Which All Black forward in 2011 became the oldest player to appear in a Rugby World Cup final?

18. Which Australian quickie was the first bowler to take a hat-trick in a Twenty20 international?

19. Which team won Ice Hockey's Elite League in 2012?
    a) Belfast Giants
    b) Cardiff Devils
    c) Sheffield Steelers

20. Which county has won the most All-Ireland Senior Gaelic Football Championships?
    a) Dublin
    b) Cork
    c) Kerry

Answers to Quiz 77: Darts

1. Leighton Rees, Richie Burnett, Marshall James, Mark Webster and Ritchie Davies
2. Nicky Virachkul
3. The Hague
4. Kirk Shepherd
5. Paul Lim
6. Les Wallace
7. Gary Mawson
8. Phill Nixon
9. Leighton Rees
10. World Grand Prix
11. Dean Winstanley
12. Steve Beaton
13. Dave Whitcombe
14. Anastasia Dobromyslova
15. Keith Deller
16. Scott Waites
17. Michael van Gerwen
18. Magnus Caris
19. John Lowe
20. Nottingham

DIFFICULT

Quiz 79: Football

1. Which German managed the Greek team that won Euro 2004?

2. Who are the six players to have won the Premier League with more than one club?

3. Who was the first goalkeeper to captain England after World War II?

4. Which two teams play their home games at the Giuseppe Meazza Stadium?

5. How many yellow cards did Wayne Rooney receive in the Premier League in the 2011/12 season?

6. Who was the only footballer to appear on Time Magazine's 100 Most Influential People in the World in 2012 list?

7. Which two countries contested the 3rd and 4th place play-off match at the 2002 World Cup?

8. Who are the two goalkeepers to save an FA Cup final penalty at Wembley?

9. Who were the four players to be sent off twice in the Premier League in 2011/12?

10. What is the Brazilian footballer Givanildo Vieira de Souza more commonly known as?

11. Which actor played Billy Bremner in the 2009 film The Damned United?

12. Who was the first Premier League footballer to score 20 goals coming off the bench?

13. Which Chelsea player missed from the spot in the 2012 Champions League final penalty shoot-out?

14. And which two Bayern Munich players missed in the same shoot-out?

15. Only three Englishmen scored more than 12 Premier League goals in 2011/12. Can you name them?

16. Who were the last Premier League team to field an all-English starting XI?

17. What was the only club not to have a player sent off in the 2011/12 Premier League season?

18. Who is the Czech Republic's all-time leading international goal scorer?

19. Who was the most fouled player in the Champions League in 2011/12?
    a) Lionel Messi
    b) Cristiano Ronaldo
    c) Franck Ribery

20. Which team received the most red cards in the Premier League in 2011/12?
    a) Bolton
    b) QPR
    c) Stoke

Answers to Quiz 78: Pot Luck

1. New Zealand
2. Port-of-Spain
3. Shivnarine Chanderpaul
4. Steve Harmison and Monty Panesar
5. 9
6. Martyn Rooney
7. Siena
8. York City
9. Luton Town
10. Tour de France
11. Pommel horse
12. Barbados
13. Brendan Dolan
14. Cyrille Regis
15. Ian Holloway
16. Kevin Pietersen
17. Brad Thorn
18. Brett Lee
19. Belfast Giants
20. Kerry

DIFFICULT

Quiz 80: Pot Luck

1. Which cabaret club hosted the World Darts Championship between 1979 and 1985?

2. What is the nickname of Gateshead's rugby league team?

3. Who is the only Indian to have scored a century and also taken five wickets in a Test match at Lord's?

4. Who was the only English player to win the Premier League Player of the Month award in 2011/12?

5. Which Irish rugby international has a sideline career as a DJ using the moniker DJ Church?

6. Who was the only player to beat Rafael Nadal in a grand slam event in 2010?

7. Brad Pitt played which baseball general manager in the 2011 film Moneyball?

8. Which Dutch rider won the 2011 Tour of Britain?

9. Who were the leading London club in the first season of the Premier League?

10. Russell Crowe starred as which heavyweight champion in the 2005 film Cinderella Man?

11. Who was the only Jamaican in the West Indies Test squad that visited England in 2012?

12. What nationality is the World Downhill skiing champion Erik Guay?

13. What was the first Irish golf club to host the Ryder Cup?

14. Which much travelled defender, who won 67 caps for Scotland, fronted a rock band called Hooligan?

15. Which country won the 2012 Africa Cup of Nations?

16. Which British-trained horse won the 2010 Prix de l'Arc de Triomphe?

17. The Velka Pardubice is a famous horse race run in which country?

18. How many English players were in the Men's Singles draw at Wimbledon in 2010?

19. In what year did the first Paralympic Games take place?
    a) 1960
    b) 1964
    c) 1968

20. A 1909 FA Cup final programme was auctioned for a record-breaking amount in 2012. How much did it sell for?
    a) £13,500
    b) £18,500
    c) £23,500

Answers to Quiz 79: Football

1. Otto Rehhagel
2. Henning Berg, Ashley Cole, Nicolas Anelka, Kolo Touré, Gaël Clichy and Carlos Tevez
3. Frank Swift
4. AC Milan and Inter Milan (it's the official name of the San Siro)
5. One
6. Lionel Messi
7. Turkey and South Korea
8. Dave Beasant and Mark Crossley
9. Mario Balotelli, Joey Barton, Djibril Cissé and David Wheater
10. Hulk
11. Stephen Graham
12. Jermain Defoe
13. Juan Mata
14. Ivica Olic and Bastian Schweinsteiger
15. Wayne Rooney, Grant Holt and Danny Graham
16. Aston Villa
17. Fulham
18. Jan Koller
19. Franck Ribéry
20. QPR

DIFFICULT

Quiz 81: Formula One

1. Who was the first winner of the Drivers' Championship?

2. Which current driver earned his only Grand Prix win to date at Monaco in 2004?

3. Who holds the record for the most Formula One starts without registering a win?

4. What is signified by a marshall waving a half black, half white flag with a car number?

5. What was the first Asian country to host a Formula One Grand Prix?

6. Who are the two drivers to have won the British Grand Prix five times?

7. Which circuit hosted the British Grand Prix in 1955, 1957, 1959, 1961 and 1962?

8. At 4.35 miles, which 2012 circuit has the longest lap length?

9. Who are the two drivers to have finished runner-up in the Drivers' Championship four times?

10. Up to the start of the 2012 season, which British driver had started the most races?

11. Which driver was killed at the 1970 Dutch Grand Prix?

12. Who is the youngest driver to start a Formula One race?

13. Who are the three men to have won the Drivers' Championship whose surname starts with a vowel?

14. Two drivers have won four races in their maiden Formula One season. Lewis Hamilton is one, who is the other?

15. Which driver's first Grand Prix victory didn't come until his 130th race in Germany in 2009?

16. In 2006, who became the youngest driver to set a Formula One fastest lap record?

17. Who holds the record for the longest wait between winning his first and second Drivers' Championships?

18. In the 1988 season, only three men won a race. Senna and Prost were two but who was the third?

19. Jenson Button won the 2011 Canadian Grand Prix despite making how many pit stops?
    a) 4
    b) 5
    c) 6

20. Who won the 1982 Drivers' Championship despite winning just one race that season?
    a) René Arnoux
    b) Didier Pironi
    c) Keke Rosberg

Answers to Quiz 80: Pot Luck

1. Jollees in Stoke-on-Trent
2. Thunder
3. Vinoo Mankad
4. Scott Parker
5. Cian Healy
6. Andy Murray
7. Billy Beane
8. Lars Boom
9. QPR
10. James J. Braddock
11. Marlon Samuels
12. Canadian
13. The K Club, Co Kildare
14. Christian Dailly
15. Zambia
16. Workforce
17. Czech Republic
18. None
19. 1960
20. £23,500

DIFFICULT

Quiz 82: Pot Luck

1. In what month does the Melbourne Cup horse race take place?

2. Which two international rugby teams compete for the Centenary Quaich?

3. In which town do the Roughyeds play rugby league?

4. Which city is the venue for the darts World Grand Prix tournament?

5. Which goalkeeper was sent off in the opening game of Euro 2012?

6. Complete the title of this golf book: Bring Me The Head of...?

7. Which city hosted the 2006 Commonwealth Games?

8. Up to and including the 2010 tournament, how many times have Brazil met Germany in the World Cup?

9. How many players are on a Canadian football team?

10. What nationality is middleweight boxing champion Sergio Gabriel Martínez?

11. Which British athletes finished first and second in the women's 400m at the 2007 World Athletics Championships?

12. Which left-handed golfer won The Masters in 2003?

13. Who was the leading goalscorer in the first season of football's Premier League?

14. Who finished second and third in the Premier League in its first season?

15. Who was the only European golfer to finish in the top ten at The Masters in 2011?

16. Which British athlete finished sixth in the women's 100m final at the 2008 Olympic Games?

17. The Hertfordshire Mavericks, Surrey Storm and Loughborough Lightning are teams in which sport?

18. What is the Brazilian midfielder Ricardo Izecson dos Santos Leite better known as?

19. How old was Amir Khan when he won the the Olympic lightweight boxing silver medal?
    a) 17
    b) 18
    c) 19

20. What is the name of Hull's Elite League ice hockey team?
    a) Hull Sharks
    b) Hull Stingrays
    c) Hull Tigers

Answers to Quiz 81: Formula One

1. Giuseppe Farina
2. Jarno Trulli
3. Andrea de Cesaris
4. Warning of unsporting behaviour
5. Japan
6. Jim Clark and Alain Prost
7. Aintree
8. Spa-Francorchamps
9. Stirling Moss and Alain Prost
10. David Coulthard
11. Piers Courage
12. Jaime Alguersuari
13. Alberto Ascari, Mario Andretti and Fernando Alonso
14. Jacques Villeneuve
15. Mark Webber
16. Nico Rosberg
17. Niki Lauda (7 years)
18. Gerhard Berger
19. 6
20. Keke Rosberg

DIFFICULT

Quiz 83: Golf

1. Which amateur shot a 65 in the opening round of the 2011 Open Championship?

2. Who won the 2009 Volvo World Matchplay title?

3. Which player made the most Open Championship appearances before winning the title?

4. Who made his Ryder Cup debut in 1974 then didn't play in the competition again until 1989?

5. Who was the last golfer to win The Open Championship in three different decades?

6. Who won the 1979 US Masters in his first appearance in the tournament?

7. Who are the three players to successfully defend the US Masters?

8. Which course hosted the only Open Championship outside England or Scotland?

9. Who was the last player to win The Open Championship on his debut appearance?

10. Who has won the most points for the American team in the history of the Ryder Cup?

11. Which course will host the 2014 Ryder Cup?

12. Who was the only Scandinavian in Europe's 2010 Ryder Cup team?

13. Rory McIlroy won the 2011 US Open at which course?

14. Which golfer's career was put in jeopardy after he almost severed his index finger in a freak boating accident in 2012?

15. Who, in 2006, became the first player to seal a Ryder Cup match by hitting a hole in one?

16. What is the name of the trophy awarded to the winner of the USPGA Championship?

17. Who was the first player to be ranked number one in the world without ever having won a major?

18. Greg Norman in 1993, Nick Price in 1994 and Tiger Woods in 2000 are the only players to manage what feat?

19. At 7,361 yards, what is the longest course to have hosted The Open Championship?
    a) Carnoustie
    b) Muirfield
    c) Turnberry

20. How many majors did Severiano Ballesteros win?
    a) 4
    b) 5
    c) 6

Answers to Quiz 82: Pot Luck

1. November
2. Scotland and Ireland
3. Oldham
4. Dublin
5. Wojciech Szczesny
6. Sergio García
7. Melbourne
8. Once
9. 12
10. Argentinean
11. Christine Ohuruogo and Nicola Sanders
12. Mike Weir
13. Teddy Sheringham
14. Aston Villa and Norwich City
15. Luke Donald
16. Jeanette Kwakye
17. Netball
18. Kaka
19. 17
20. Hull Stingrays

DIFFICULT

Quiz 84: Pot Luck

1. Who was Britain's last speedway World Champion?

2. The Larry O'Brien Trophy is awarded to the winning team in which competition?

3. Who was the only New Zealander to feature in the rugby union Heineken Cup final in 2011?

4. What name connects a former Southampton and Arsenal midfielder and a one-time caddy of Tiger Woods?

5. What is the only chaser to win the Scottish, Welsh and Aintree Grand National?

6. Which 2011/12 Premier League manager had a spell as the British Virgin Islands' technical director of football in 2000?

7. What was the venue of the first Winter Olympic Games?

8. Leeds, Sunderland, Reading and Republic of Ireland defender Ian Harte had a spell with which Spanish club?

9. What was the last French-bred horse to win the Grand National?

10. Willie Park Sr was the first winner of which sporting event?

11. Who rode Homecoming Queen to victory in the 2012 1,000 Guineas?

12. Which Brazilian won the World Cup as a player in 1958 and 1962 and as a manager in 1970?

13. Who were the four members of Britain's 1991 World Championship winning 4x400m relay team?

14. Which Australian golfer shot a 59 at the Greenbriar Classic on the US PGA Tour in 2010?

15. Graeme Souness had managerial spells at which three continental European clubs?

16. The figure of Abe Mitchell sits on the top of which famous sporting trophy?

17. Which Swiss rider won the 2010 Tour of Britain cycle race?

18. The Wooden Award is a prize given to outstanding players in which sport?

19. How many times did Arnold Palmer win the US Open?
    a) never
    b) once
    c) twice

20. The longest winning streak by the England rugby union team in 2002 and 2003 stretched for how many matches?
    a) 13
    b) 14
    c) 15

Answers to Quiz 83: Golf

1. Tom Lewis
2. Ross Fisher
3. Darren Clarke
4. Christy O'Connor Jr
5. Gary Player in 1959, 1968 and 1974
6. Fuzzy Zoeller
7. Jack Nicklaus, Nick Faldo and Tiger Woods
8. Royal Portrush
9. Ben Curtis
10. Billy Casper
11. Gleneagles
12. Peter Hanson
13. Congressional CC
14. Jesper Parnevik
15. Paul Casey
16. Wanamaker Trophy
17. Lee Westwood
18. Hit four rounds of under 70 while winning The Open Championship
19. Carnoustie
20. 5

DIFFICULT

Quiz 85: Horse Racing

1. The father of which contemporary jockey rode the winner of the 2,000 Guineas in 1975 and 1976?

2. Which track hosted The Derby between 1914 and 1918 and 1940 and 1945?

3. Which 100/1 outsider won the 1990 Cheltenham Gold Cup?

4. What was the last mare to win the Grand National?

5. The Dubai World Cup is run at which course?

6. What was the only grey horse to win the Grand National in the 20th century?

7. Who was the first female rider to ride 100 flat winners during a calendar year?

8. Which 100/1 outsider won the 1967 Grand National?

9. How old was Lester Piggott when he won his first race?

10. What is the most easterly racecourse in Britain?

11. The brilliant Best Mate died suddenly in a 2005 race at which course?

12. In which Irish county is Fairyhouse Racecourse?

13. What horse won the 2010 Welsh Grand National?

14. Denman was defeated over hurdles just once. Which horse inflicted that defeat?

15. Which foreign-born jockey won the Derby on High-Rise in 1998 and the 2,000 Guineas in 2007 on Cockney Rebel?

16. Which Derby winner is the sire of wonder horse Frankel?

17. In 1989, the St Leger was run away from its usual home. Which course staged the race?

18. Can you name the nine racecourses located in Yorkshire?

19. What is the oldest racecourse in England?
    a) Chester
    b) Newmarket
    c) York

20. How old was jockey Dick Saunders when he won the 1982 Grand National on Grittar?
    a) 46
    b) 47
    c) 48

Answers to Quiz 84: Pot Luck

1. Mark Loram
2. The NBA finals
3. Mark Sorenson
4. Steve Williams
5. Earth Summit
6. André Villas-Boas
7. Chamonix
8. Levante
9. Neptunes Collonges
10. The Open Championship
11. Ryan Moore
12. Mario Zagallo
13. Roger Black, Derek Redmond, John Regis and Kriss Akabusi
14. Stuart Appleby
15. Benfica, Torino and Galatasaray
16. The Ryder Cup
17. Michael Albasini
18. Basketball
19. Once
20. 14

DIFFICULT

Quiz 86: Pot Luck

1. Dun Whinny, Denty Den and Wee Bogle are holes at which Scottish golf course?

2. Which American basketball star is a part-owner of Liverpool Football Club?

3. In 1977, Charlotte Brew became the first woman to do what?

4. The Val Barker Trophy is awarded to the most stylish performer in which Olympic discipline?

5. Which Croat was the leading goal scorer at the 1998 World Cup?

6. Up to 2012, six countries had hosted both the Summer and Winter Olympics. Name them.

7. Which swimmer carried the British flag at the opening ceremony of the 2008 Olympic Games?

8. Which jockey won The Derby on Sinndar in 2000, High Chaparral in 2002 and Motivator in 2005?

9. Which two rugby union teams compete for the Babcock Trophy?

10. Which British Formula One driver has had the most podium finishes?

11. Which two countries were involved in a controversial 1956 Olympic water polo match dubbed 'Blood in the Water'?

12. Which country was originally chosen to host the 1986 World Cup but withdrew for financial reasons?

13. Who was the first British golfer to win The Masters?

14. Which male dart player was beaten by Anastasia Dobromyslova in the 2009 Grand Slam of Darts?

15. Which city hosted the 1932 Summer Olympics?

16. On 18 May 1958, Maria Teresa de Filippis became the first woman to do what?

17. In which American city will you find an NHL team called the Mighty Ducks?

18. Which three players captained Wales during their 2012 Six Nations Rugby Grand Slam?

19. Which county has won the most All Ireland Senior Hurling Championships?
    a) Kilkenny
    b) Limerick
    c) Tipperary

20. The Leigh Matthews Trophy is awarded to the most valuable player in which sport?
    a) American football
    b) Australian rules football
    c) Gaelic football

Answers to Quiz 85: Horse Racing

1. Frankie Dettori (his father is Gianfranco)
2. Newmarket
3. Norton's Coin
4. Nickel Coin
5. Meydan Racecourse
6. Nicolaus Silver
7. Hayley Turner
8. Foinavon
9. 12
10. Great Yarmouth
11. Exeter
12. Meath
13. Synchronised
14. Nicanor
15. Olivier Peslier
16. Galileo
17. Ayr
18. Beverley, Catterick, Doncaster, Pontefract, Redcar, Ripon, Thirsk, Wetherby and York
19. Chester
20. 48

DIFFICULT

Quiz 87: Motorsport

1. The winner of which event is awarded the Borg-Warner Trophy?

2. The opening race of the 2012 Moto GP season took place in which country?

3. Which Briton in 1995 became the youngest winner of the World Rally Championship Drivers' title?

4. Which English rider won the 2011 British Superbikes Championship?

5. Which American finished just two points behind him in the standings?

6. What was the first country outside Europe to host an event in the Speedway Grand Prix series?

7. Which British Superbikes rider shares a name with a former Irish rugby international?

8. Which driver holds the record for accumulating the most Formula One points without registering a win?

9. Over how many laps is the Indianapolis 500 run?

10. Which Briton won the World Rally Championship in 2001?

11. Which Italian won seven consecutive 500cc World Motorcycle Riders' Championship titles between 1966 and 1972?

12. Who was the only woman to race in the 2011 and 2012 Moto2 Championship?

13. Which German-born racer is the only driver to posthumously win the Formula One World Drivers' Championship?

14. Which British brothers won the 2009 World Sidecar Championship?

15. In which sport was the Craven Shield awarded?

16. Which British driver started 22nd on the grid in the 1983 US Grand Prix West but went on to record a spectacular win?

17. What colour flag is flown to show that riders are starting the last lap of a speedway race?

18. The 2005, 2006 and 2007 World Touring Car Championship Drivers' championships were won by which British driver?

19. Which Scot was part of the Le Mans 24 Hours race winning team in 2008?

20. Who won Speedway's Elite League Riders' Championship in 2011?
    a) Rory Schlein
    b) Leigh Adams
    c) Jason Crump

Answers to Quiz 86: Pot Luck

1. Gleneagles
2. Lebron James
3. Ride in the Grand National
4. Boxing
5. Davor Suker
6. France, USA, Italy, Canada, Germany and Japan
7. Mark Foster
8. Johnny Murtagh
9. British Army and the Royal Navy
10. David Coulthard
11. USSR and Hungary
12. Colombia
13. Sandy Lyle
14. Vincent van der Voort
15. Los Angeles
16. Drive in a Formula One Grand Prix
17. Anaheim
18. Sam Warburton, Ryan Jones and Gethin Jenkins
19. Kilkenny
20. Australian rules football

DIFFICULT

Quiz 88: Pot Luck

1. Which snooker player can play the oboe and was also a budding leg spinner for the London Schools cricket team?

2. The Tingle Creek horse racing meeting is run at which course?

3. Who is South Africa's leading international rugby union point scorer?

4. Who is the only player to score 6 tries in a single rugby league Super League match?

5. At which Olympics were starting blocks used for the first time?

6. Briton James Willstrop is a world number one performer in which sport?

7. The Spanish football club Levante are based in which city?

8. St Leo is the middle name of which record-breaking sprinter?

9. Who is the only Canadian golfer to win The Masters?

10. Who won Britain's only medal at the 2006 Winter Olympics in the Women's skeleton?

11. How many teams took part in the men's Olympic football competition at the 2012 Games?

12. Why was Jessica Ennis's personal best time in the 100m hurdles at the Great City Games in 2012 ruled invalid?

13. Which Frenchman scored the first ever World Cup golden goal against Paraguay in 1998?

14. Who made his Champions League debut in the 2012 final?

15. Briton Malcolm Cooper won Olympic gold at which sport?

16. Which Spanish team did Bayern Munich beat in the 2001 Champions League final?

17. Mario Lemieux, Phil Esposito and Mark Messier were legendary performers in which sport?

18. Which country won baseball gold at the 2008 Olympic Games?

19. Scotsman Lawrence Tynes is a successful player in which American sport?
    a) American football
    b) baseball
    c) basketball

20. Who was the first male tennis player to complete the Grand Slam and win an Olympic Games gold medal?
    a) Andre Agassi
    b) Stefan Edberg
    c) Pete Sampras

Answers to Quiz 87: Motorsport

1. Indy 500
2. Qatar
3. Colin McRae
4. Tommy Hill
5. John Hopkins
6. New Zealand
7. Shane Byrne
8. Nick Heidfeld
9. 200
10. Richard Burns
11. Giacomo Agostini
12. Elena Rosell
13. Jochen Rindt
14. Tom and Ben Birchall
15. Speedway
16. John Watson
17. Yellow with a black diagonal cross
18. Andy Priaulx
19. Allan McNish
20. Rory Schlein

DIFFICULT

Quiz 89: Olympic Games

1. What is the lightest weight division in men's Olympic boxing?

2. Which barefoot runner won the 1960 Olympic marathon?

3. What was the first event of the 2012 London Olympics?

4. Who was the first black swimmer to win an Olympic gold medal?

5. Which country did he represent?

6. Tennis player Andre Agassi's father boxed for which country in the 1948 Olympics?

7. Which Premier League footballer was the leading goal scorer in the 2004 Olympic men's football tournament?

8. The Albatross is the nickname of which giant, German, triple gold medal winning swimmer?

9. James Cleveland are the real first names of which Olympic legend?

10. London Marathon founder Chris Brasher won Olympic gold in which athletics event?

11. What are the only two countries other than USA or USSR to have won gold in Olympic men's basketball?

12. Waldi the dachshund, the first Olympic mascot, appeared at which Games?

13. Which two sports were part of the 2008 Olympics but were discontinued for 2012?

14. What is the only country to host the Summer Olympics but not win a gold medal at those Games?

15. In 1932, American Eddie Eagan became the first man to do what?

16. Who was the first winner of the Tour de France to win an Olympic gold medal?

17. What colour is the middle ring on the top row of the Olympic flag?

18. Which city hosted the equestrian events at the 1956 Olympics?

19. In 1904, George Eyser won gymnastic gold despite what disability?
    a) he was blind
    b) he had an artificial leg
    c) he was deaf

20. How many gold medals did Michael Phelps win at the 2004 and 2008 Games?
    a) 12
    b) 14
    c) 16

Answers to Quiz 88: Pot Luck

1. Peter Ebdon
2. Sandown
3. Percy Montgomery
4. Lesley Vainikolo
5. London 1948
6. Squash
7. Valencia
8. Usain Bolt
9. Mike Weir
10. Shelley Rudman
11. 16
12. There were only 9 hurdles on the track instead of ten
13. Laurent Blanc
14. Ryan Betrand
15. Shooting
16. Valencia
17. Ice hockey
18. South Korea
19. American football
20. Andre Agassi

DIFFICULT

Quiz 90: Pot Luck

1. The Nunthorpe Stakes is run at which racecourse?

2. Who won the BBC Overseas Sports Personality of the Year award in 2011?

3. Who is the leading point scorer in the history of international rugby union?

4. In what sport can a player win The Albert Goldthorpe Medal?

5. Who played for the Barbarians in a rugby union game against Australia at Twickenham in 2011 despite never having played the 15-man code before?

6. Excluding St Andrews, which course has hosted the Open Championship the most times?

7. Which American city was originally awarded the 1976 Winter Olympics but didn't host the Games after residents voted against it?

8. What is the only city to have hosted the World Athletics Championship twice?

9. Who chipped in from off the green in a play-off to win the 1987 Masters?

10. Comiskey Park and Wrigley Field are baseball parks in which American city?

11. Briton David Florence won a silver medal at the 2008 Olympics in which sport?

12. Andrew Flintoff had a brief spell in the Indian Premier League with which team?

13. In 2002, Steve Bradbury won Australia's first ever gold medal at the Winter Olympics. In which sport?

14. Which Briton won a silver medal in the women's 1,500m at the 2009 World Athletics Championships?

15. Who is the only snooker player to win the BBC Sports Personality of the Year award?

16. Which 46-year old became the oldest man to win a world boxing title after winning the WBC light heavyweight championship in 2011?

17. In what year did the Summer and Winter Olympics last take place in the same year?

18. The main road into the city of Hull is named after which rugby league legend?

19. James Connolly won the first ever Olympic gold medal. In what event did he compete?
    a) high jump
    b) long jump
    c) triple jump

20. In what year were floodlights first installed at Murrayfield Stadium?
    a) 1974
    b) 1984
    c) 1994

Answers to Quiz 89: Olympic Games

1. Light flyweight
2. Abebe Bikila
3. Women's football
4. Anthony Nesty
5. Suriname
6. Iran
7. Carlos Tevez
8. Michael Gross
9. Jesse Owens
10. 3000m steeplechase
11. Yugoslavia and Argentina
12. Munich 1972
13. Baseball and softball
14. Canada (Montreal 1976)
15. Win gold medals in the Summer and Winter Olympics
16. Miguel Indurain
17. Black
18. Stockholm (quarantine laws prevented Melbourne from hosting the event)
19. He had an artificial leg
20. 14

DIFFICULT

Quiz 91: Rugby League

1. What was the venue for the 2009 Super League game between Catalan Dragons and Warrington Wolves?

2. Who was named man of the match in the 2011 Super League Grand Final?

3. Which team won the first Super League match in 1996?

4. The Whitebank Stadium is the home ground of which team?

5. Who, in 2004, set the record for the most tries in a Super League season?

6. Bradford Bulls ran up a Super League record score of 96 in 2000 against which team?

7. Who was the first player to score over 300 points in a season in top-flight competitions in Australia and England?

8. Who is the only player to score four tries in a Challenge Cup final?

9. Who captained The Exiles team in their 2011 game against England?

10. Gareth Hock received a five-match ban for an eye gouge on which player?

11. Who was sent off in the 1993 Challenge Cup final?

12. Can you name three Wigan players to have scored five tries in a Super League game?

13. Who scored a hat-trick for Warrington in the 2010 Challenge Cup final?

14. Which team won their only World Club Challenge against Canberra Raiders in 1989?

15. Who scored a record-equalling 20 points in the 1999 Challenge Cup final?

16. Who, in 1994, became the youngest player to appear in a Challenge Cup final?

17. Who was the first British player to win 50 international caps?

18. What unwanted record was set by Hull's Paul Rose in a 1983 game?

19. Which ground hosted the 1991 World Club Challenge?
    a) Anfield
    b) Maine Road
    c) Bramall Lane

20. A team called the Rebels will join Championship 1 in 2013. In what town will they be based?
    a) Northampton
    b) Oxford
    c) Swindon

Answers to Quiz 90: Pot Luck

1. York
2. Novak Djokovic
3. Dan Carter
4. Rugby league
5. Sam Tomkins
6. Prestwick
7. Denver
8. Helsinki
9. Larry Mize
10. Chicago
11. Canoeing
12. Chennai Super Kings
13. Speed skating
14. Lisa Dobriskey
15. Steve Davis
16. Bernard Hopkins
17. 1992
18. Clive Sullivan
19. Triple jump
20. 1994

DIFFICULT

Quiz 92: Pot Luck

1. Which tennis player was presented with a 1,760lb cow called Juliette after winning his first Wimbledon title?

2. Which Irish international made 56 appearances in the then Five Nations Championship between 1964 and 1979?

3. The Kumuls is the nickname of which international rugby league team?

4. Who was given a section of the Berlin Wall in honour of his performances at the 2009 World Athletics Championships?

5. Angel Cabrera was the second Argentine golfer to win a major. Who, in 1967, was the first?

6. Who are the three people to win the BBC Sports Personality of the Year award twice?

7. Which country won the 2011 women's football World Cup?

8. The Eagles are a speedway team in which English town?

9. Over what distance are Olympic rowing races contested?

10. Who was the performance director of Great Britain's all-conquering 2008 Olympic cycling team?

11. Kirsty Coventry is an Olympic champion swimmer from which country?

12. Who was the first player to score 100 points in an NBA basketball game?

13. Al Ahly versus Zamalek is a football derby in which city?

14. Ravi Bopara played in the Indian Premier League for which side?

15. Who were the six Britons to win multiple medals at the 2008 Olympics?

Answers – page 191

16. Who is Sri Lanka's leading Test match run scorer?

17. Which Samoan rugby player was nicknamed 'The Chiropractor'?

18. What sport takes place in a dohyō?

19. How old was Martina Navratilova when she made her Olympic debut?
    a) 37
    b) 42
    c) 47

20. How many consecutive matches did the England rugby union team lose between February and November 2006?
    a) 5
    b) 6
    c) 7

Answers to Quiz 91: Rugby League

1. Barcelona's Olympic Stadium
2. Rob Burrow
3. Paris St Germain
4. Oldham
5. Lesley Vainikolo
6. Salford
7. Brett Hodgson
8. Leroy Rivett
9. Danny Buderus
10. Ben Harrison
11. Richard Eyres
12. Jason Robinson, Tony Smith and Pat Richards
13. Chris Hicks
14. Widnes
15. Iestyn Harris
16. Francis Cummins
17. Adrian Morley
18. He was the first player sent to the sin bin in a Challenge Cup final
19. Anfield
20. Northampton

DIFFICULT

Quiz 93: Rugby Union

1. Which team won their first Super 15 title in 2011?

2. Which two countries compete for the Antim Cup?

3. Who has won the most caps for the British and Irish Lions?

4. Where do the Newport Gwent Dragons play their home games?

5. In what country was French legend Serge Blanco born?

6. Which two Super 15 teams met at Twickenham in March 2011?

7. In what year did Italy join the Six Nations Championship?

8. Two players have scored 400 points for England. Jonny Wilkinson is one. Can you name the other?

9. Who won the man of the match award in the 2011 Heineken Cup final?

10. Who are the two French players with over 100 international caps?

11. Who won the Heineken Cup with London Wasps in 2007 and Leinster in 2011?

12. Which three players were part of the Welsh Grand Slam winning teams of 2005, 2008 and 2012?

13. Who are the five Englishmen to have scored at least 30 international tries?

14. How many Welsh forwards scored a try during their 2012 Grand Slam winning campaign?

15. Who were the joint leading try scorers at the 2011 Rugby World Cup?

16. Who is the only player to win two Heineken Cup final man of the match awards?

17. Which Leinster forward is the oldest player to win the Heineken Cup?

18. Who is the only Frenchman to have scored over 200 points in the Six Nations Championship?

19. What is the largest margin of victory in a Six Nations match?
    a) 37 points
    b) 47 points
    c) 57 points

20. Which team holds the record for the most successive international defeats?
    a) France
    b) Scotland
    c) Wales

Answers to Quiz 92: Pot Luck

DIFFICULT

Quiz 94: Pot Luck

1. Brian Vitori, Greg Lamb and Kyle Jarvis play international cricket for which country?

2. In 1995, who became the only rugby union player to win the BBC Overseas Sports Personality of the Year award?

3. Which American did Richard Krajicek beat in the 1996 Wimbledon Men's Singles final?

4. Can you name the two Irish rugby union players to have scored over 500 international points?

5. Leslie Law won Olympic gold for Britain in 2004 in which sport?

6. Which Irishman left Celtic for Spartak Moscow in 2010?

7. Which South Korean golfer won the 2009 US PGA Championship?

8. Which wicket-keeper holds the record for the most dismissals in the history of Test cricket?

9. Hoosiers is a film about which sport?

10. In 2012, who became the first team in 11 years to beat Manchester United and Arsenal in back to back matches?

11. Who were the last team to manage the same feat before them in 2001?

12. Which horse won the 1956 Grand National after Devon Loch's famous stumble?

13. Who scored England's first goal at Wembley during Roy Hodgson's managerial reign?

14. Who were the last winners of the Home Nations Football Championship?

15. Which Irish swimmer won three gold medals at the 1996 Olympics?

16. The Hillary Shield is awarded to the winner of rugby union internationals between which two teams?

17. Who are the two drivers to win the World Drivers' Championship in only their second season?

18. Which snooker player recorded a version of the David Cassidy song I Am A Clown?

19. Which team conceded just one penalty in the 2011/12 Premier League season?

20. Tommi Makkinen, Petter Solberg and Juha Kankunnen have been world champions at which sport?
    a) rally driving
    b) speedway
    c) ski jumping

21. Benjamin Boukpeti became Togo's first Olympic gold medal winner at the 2008 games. In what event was he competing?
    a) badminton
    b) canoeing
    c) sailing

Answers to Quiz 93: Rugby Union

1. Queensland Reds
2. Georgia and Romania
3. Willie John McBride
4. Rodney Parade
5. Venezuela
6. Sharks and Crusaders
7. 2000
8. Paul Grayson
9. Jonathan Sexton
10. Fabien Pelous and Philippe Sella
11. Eoin Reddan
12. Gethin Jenkins, Adam Jones and Ryan Jones
13. Jason Robinson, Ben Cohen, Will Greenwood, Jeremy Guscott and Rory Underwood
14. None
15. Chris Ashton and Vincent Clerc
16. Austin Healy
17. Brad Thorn
18. Dimitri Yachvili
19. 57 points by England against Italy in 2001
20. France (they once lost 18 in a row)

DIFFICULT

Quiz 95: Snooker

1. Who was the last player to win the World Championship on his debut appearance?

2. Before Judd Trump beat Mark Allen at the 2011 UK Open, the last all left-handed ranking event final was the 1989 British Open. Who were the two finalists?

3. Which Essex pro claimed his first major tournament when taking the 2011 Australian Open?

4. Who is the only South African to reach the World Snooker Championship final in the Crucible era?

5. Which card-playing snooker pro won the second Poker Million?

6. Who scored a century in just 3m 31s at the 1996 UK Championship?

7. Which Canadian reached the semi-final of the World Championship in 1980 and 1984?

8. Name the three players who made their debut at the World Championship in 2012?

9. Which snooker player is an expert on equine breeding?

10. Who won the women's World Championship for the seventh time in 2011?

11. Which player sat in for Jarvis Cocker to host a prog-rock show on radio station BBC 6 Music?

12. Who did Steve Davis beat to claim his first World Championship?

13. Which country won the 2011 Snooker World Cup?

14. Why did 22-year-old Diane Philips make the headlines at the 2000 British Open?

15. The man credited with inventing the game of snooker shares a name with which British Prime Minister?

16. Jimmy White is from which area of south London?

17. Who scored a record-breaking six centuries in a 2011 World Championship match?

18. Who is the only player to score a century break in his first ever frame at the World Championship?

19. Which Irish city hosted the Finals of the Players Tour Championship 2011/2012?
    a) Cork
    b) Galway
    c) Limerick

20. Which player wasn't mentioned in the Chas n Dave classic Snooker Loopy?
    a) Terry Griffiths
    b) Alex Higgins
    c) Willie Thorne

Answers to Quiz 94: Pot Luck

1. Zimbabwe
2. Jonah Lomu
3. MaliVai Washington
4. Ronan O'Gara and David Humphreys
5. Equestrianism - Individual eventing
6. Aiden McGeady
7. Yang Yong-eun
8. Mark Boucher
9. Basketball
10. Wigan Athletic
11. Southampton
12. ESB
13. Danny Welbeck
14. Northern Ireland
15. Michelle Smith
16. New Zealand and England
17. Jacques Villeneuve and Lewis Hamilton
18. Peter Ebdon
19. Tottenham Hotspur
20. Rally driving
21. Canoeing

DIFFICULT

Quiz 96: Pot Luck

1. Who are the two New Zealanders to have won a golf major?

2. Which French tennis player is nicknamed Genius in honour of her impressive IQ of 175?

3. Baby-Foot, Csosco and Bordfodbold are other names for what game?

4. Which famous actor's father won gold in the rowing coxless pairs at the 1948 Olympics?

5. In what sport do players compete for the Weber Cup?

6. In 1993, which 51-year-old became the oldest player to take part in golf's Ryder Cup?

7. Which New Zealander was the first man to score over 1,000 runs in Twenty20 international cricket?

8. The Birmingham Road End is a stand at which English football ground?

9. The Hurricane was a 1999 film about which boxer?

10. Which American beat Phillips Idowu to gold in the triple jump at the 2011 World Athletics Championships?

11. Jan Verhaas and Zhu Ying are referees in which sport?

12. In which American city is an NBA team called the Timberwolves based?

13. Which football club had a top ten hit with a version of Donna Summer's Hot Stuff?

14. What are the three countries to have won the Women's Rugby World Cup?

15. What will be the venue for the 2018 Commonwealth Games?

16. Which Irish rugby union player was born in Tiberias, Israel?

17. Who has scored Premier League goals for West Ham, Aston Villa, Nottingham Forest and Blackpool?

18. Which Australian had scored over 15,000 first-class runs before finally making his Test debut?

19. Which country will host the Ryder Cup in 2016?
    a) France
    b) Germany
    c) Spain

20. Which American World War Two general appeared in the pentathlon at the 1912 Olympics?
    a) Eisenhower
    b) Patton
    c) MacArthur

Answers to Quiz 95: Snooker

1. Terry Griffiths
2. Dean Reynolds and Tony Meo
3. Stuart Bingham
4. Perrie Mans
5. Jimmy White
6. Tony Drago
7. Kirk Stevens
8. Jamie Jones, Cao Yupeng and Luca Brecel
9. Peter Ebdon
10. Reanne Evans
11. Steve Davis
12. Doug Mountjoy
13. China
14. She did a topless streak
15. Neville Chamberlain
16. Tooting
17. Mark Selby
18. Fergal O'Brien
19. Galway
20. Alex Higgins

DIFFICULT

Quiz 97: Tennis

1. In 2010, which two players were involved in the longest ever match at Wimbledon?

2. What was the score in the final set of that match?

3. Which ATP event is played on blue clay?

4. What happened in the 2009 Wimbledon match between Amélie Mauresmo and Dinara Safina that had never happened before?

5. Who, in 2007, became the only player not seeded in the top 16 to win the Wimbledon Ladies' Singles title?

6. Which tennis player appeared in Time Magazine's list of the 100 Most Influential People in the World in 2012?

7. Who is the only Brazilian man to win a Grand Slam singles title?

8. What nationality is Stanislas Wawrinka?

9. Who was the first Swede to win the Australian Open in the open era?

10. Who are the two players, one American and one Australian, to win Grand Slam titles as a teenager, in their 20s and in their 30s?

11. Who was Wimbledon's last amateur Men's Singles winner?

12. Who succeeded John Lloyd as the captain of the Great Britain Davis Cup team in 2010?

13. Which Wimbledon champion said, 'Eighty per cent of the women playing at Wimbledon are lazy, fat pigs and shouldn't be allowed on the show courts'?

14. Which Chilean did Rafael Nadal beat in the 2008 Olympic tennis final?

15. Who became the first mother to win a Grand Slam event since 1980 when she won the 2009 US Open?

16. What were used at Wimbledon for the first time in 1986?

17. Who, in 2010, became the first Italian woman to win a Grand Slam title after beating Samantha Stosur in the French Open final?

18. Prior to Tim Henman, who was the last British male to reach a Wimbledon semi-final?

19. Who won the most Grand Slam titles out of
    a) Boris Becker
    b) Ivan Lendl
    c) John McEnroe

20. Novak Djokovic went unbeaten for how many matches at the start of 2011?
    a) 41
    b) 42
    c) 43

Answers to Quiz 96: Pot Luck

1. Bob Charles and Michael Campbell
2. Marion Bartoli
3. Table football
4. Hugh Laurie (his father was Ran Laurie)
5. Ten-pin bowling
6. Raymond Floyd
7. Brendon McCullum
8. The Hawthorns
9. Rubin Carter
10. Christian Taylor
11. Snooker
12. Minnesota
13. Arsenal
14. New Zealand, England and USA
15. Gold Coast, Australia
16. Jamie Heaslip
17. Marlon Harewood
18. Michael Hussey
19. France
20. Patton

DIFFICULT

Quiz 98: Pot Luck

1. Which South African took 100 wickets in the fewest number of Test matches?

2. Which World Cup winner had a brief spell at Birmingham City in 2003/04?

3. World Champion 400m runner Kirani James is from which Caribbean country?

4. Which African politician said, 'Cricket civilises people and creates good gentlemen'?

5. Which Norwegian-born jockey rode the winner of the St Leger in both 2010 and 2011?

6. What are the three divisions of the NBA's Eastern Conference?

7. What nationality is tennis player Milos Raonic?

8. Which three teams didn't win a single point in the group stage of the 2011/12 Champions League?

9. Which French winger, who was also the first captain to lift the Heineken Cup, scored a hat-trick of tries against Wales in 1999 but still ended up on the losing side?

10. Which British athlete won a silver medal in the 800m at the 2008 European Athletics Championships?

11. What was two-time European Cup winner Garry Birtles' occupation before he was signed by Brian Clough at Nottingham Forest?

12. Who won the BBC Sports Personality of the Year Coach Award in 2009?

13. Which British Olympic 400m runner is now the co-owner of an Isle of Man TT motorcycle team?

14. Which Scottish athlete won a bronze medal in the women's 3,000m at the 1988 Olympic Games?

15. Which country knocked England out of the 2011 Women's World Cup?

16. What is the connection between the presidency of John F Kennedy and the 2012 winner of the 1,000 Guineas horse race?

17. Which Swiss player won the Men's Singles at the 1992 Olympic Tennis tournament?

18. What name connects a former Hull City manager and a British 400m relay specialist?

19. Who was the first Australian to make a century in home and away Test debuts?
    a) Michael Clarke
    b) Mike Hussey
    c) Ricky Ponting

20. Which country did not appear in the first ever modern Olympic Games?
    a) Bulgaria
    b) Chile
    c) Russia

Answers to Quiz 97: Tennis

1. John Isner and Nicolas Mahut
2. 70-68
3. ATP Madrid Masters
4. It was the first match played under Wimbledon's new roof
5. Venus Williams
6. Novak Djokovic
7. Gustavo Kuerten
8. Swiss
9. Mats Wilander
10. Ken Rosewall and Pete Sampras
11. John Newcombe
12. Leon Smith
13. Richard Krajicek
14. Fernando González
15. Kim Clijsters
16. Yellow balls
17. Francesca Schiavone
18. Roger Taylor
19. Ivan Lendl with 8
20. 42

DIFFICULT

Quiz 99: US Sports

1. Who were the first NFL team to win a regular season game at Wembley?

2. What was the former name of the Oklahoma City Thunder?

3. Who is the all-time leading rusher in NFL history?

4. The opening game of the 2012 baseball season was played in which country?

5. Quarterback Kurt Warner played for which three NFL franchises?

6. Name the four NFL teams that have lost four Super Bowls.

7. Which Olympic legend was drafted by the Chicago Bulls but never played a game in the NBA?

8. Which ice hockey team has won the NHL's Stanley Cup the most times?

9. What is the name of the award given to the best pitcher in baseball?

10. Who is the youngest Super Bowl winning quarterback in NFL history?

11. Excluding the New York Yankees, which team has won the World Series the most times?

12. What are the four NFL teams that have never appeared in the Super Bowl?

13. Who has thrown the most touchdown passes in the history of the NFL?

14. The Round Mound of Rebound was the nickname of which basketball player?

15. Which sprinter is the only man with an Olympic gold medal and a Super Bowl ring?

16. Denver Broncos legend John Elway was originally drafted by which team?

17. Which stadium has hosted the Super Bowl the most times?

18. What name is given to the last player selected in the NFL draft?

19. NBA star Lebron James launched a pair of trainers inspired by which English football club?
    a) Arsenal
    b) Liverpool
    c) Manchester United

20. What is the nickname of NFL wide receiver Calvin Johnson?
    a) Automan
    b) Megatron
    c) Superman

Answers to Quiz 98: Pot Luck

1. Dale Steyn
2. Christophe Dugarry
3. Grenada
4. Robert Mugabe
5. William Buick
6. Atlantic, Central and Southeast
7. Canadian
8. Villarreal, FC Otelul Galati and Dinamo Zagreb
9. Emile Ntamack
10. Michael Rimmer
11. Carpet fitter
12. Fabio Capello
13. Derek Redmond
14. Yvonne Murray
15. France
16. Camelot won the race. Camelot was also the nickname of JFK's presidency
17. Marc Rosset
18. Phil Brown
19. Michael Clarke
20. Russia

DIFFICULT

Quiz 100: Pot Luck

1. Olympic swimmer Eric 'The Eel' Moussambani represented which country?

2. Which two French teams met in the final of rugby union's 2012 Amlin Challenge Cup?

3. Which current Australian batsman was involved in 8 run outs in his first 35 Test matches?

4. Which team won the French football championship for the first time in 2012?

5. Who trained the winner of both the 1,000 Guineas and 2,000 Guineas in 2012?

6. Frankie Dettori won his first Derby in 2007 on which horse?

7. Which Scot is the manager of the MLS side Portland Timbers?

8. Which four African countries made their World Cup debut at the 2006 tournament in Germany?

9. Gillian Coultard is England's most capped player in which sport?

10. The film Murderball was about which sport?

11. How many players are there in a water polo team?

12. What was unique about the 1973 Five Nations Rugby Championship?

13. Bryan Clay won which athletics event at the 2008 Olympics?

14. Which Irishman was named rugby union's European Player of the Year in 2012?

15. Which country lost in the final of the Davis Cup in 1981, 2006, 2008, 2011?

16. Which two African countries made their Rugby World Cup debut in 1995?

17. Malaysia's Safuan Said is a world champion in which sport?

18. Which Australian was the last man out in England's historic 2-run win over Australia at Edgbaston in the 2005 Ashes?

19. How old was Sir Steve Redgrave when he won his last Olympic gold medal?
    a) 37
    b) 38
    c) 39

20. The Bill Russell Most Valuable Player Award is awarded in which sport?
    a) baseball
    b) basketball
    c) ice hockey

Answers to Quiz 99: US Sports

1. New York Giants
2. Seattle Supersonics
3. Emmit Smith
4. Japan
5. St Louis Rams, New York Giants and Arizona Cardinals
6. Buffalo Bills, Denver Broncos, Minnesota Vikings and New England Patriots
7. Carl Lewis
8. Montreal Canadiens
9. The Cy Young Award
10. Ben Roethlisberger
11. St Louis Cardinals
12. Cleveland Browns, Detroit Lions, Jacksonville Jaguars and Houston Texans
13. Brett Favre
14. Charles Barkley
15. Bob Hayes
16. Baltimore Colts
17. Louisiana Superdome
18. Mr Irrelevant
19. Liverpool
20. Megatron

DIFFICULT

Keeping Score

Keeping Score

Keeping Score

Keeping Score

Keeping Score

Keeping Score

Keeping Score

Keeping Score

Keeping Score

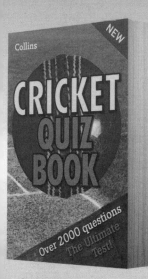
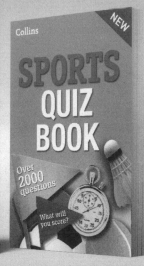
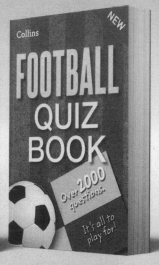